D0540274

Mission After Christendom

David Smith

DARTON · LONGMAN + TODD

First published in 2003 by
Darton, Longman and Todd Ltd
1 Spencer Court
140–142 Wandsworth High Street
London SW18 4JJ

The right of David Smith to be identified as the Author of this work has been
asserted in accordance with the Copyright, Designs and Patents Act 1988.

ISBN 0–232–52483–1

A catalogue record for this book is available from the British Library.

Designed by Sandie Boccacci
Phototypeset in 9/12.25pt Utopia by Intype London Ltd
Printed and bound in Great Britain by
Page Bros, Norwich, Norfolk

Contents

List of Illustrations

Foreword

'The church must forever be asking "What kind of day is it today?"'
wrote one of the more prophetic theologians of the last generation, 'for
no two days are alike in her history.' Dr Smith is a prophet too, and in
this profound book he raises that same question provocatively and
answers it convincingly.

Any useful answer will involve an examination of contemporary
Western culture and its antecedents. It also needs to explore both a
world situation where Western habits of thought still swing between desiring to dictate to the non-Western world and ignoring it
altogether, and the state of a church which in the course of a century
has been transformed from a predominantly Western entity to one
in which Africans, Asians and Latin Americans form the majority. And
no answer would be satisfactory that did not mine Scripture and the
Christian tradition, bringing out of that treasury things new and
old.

Dr Smith has done all these things. His analysis of contemporary
Western culture and its historical roots is disturbing, but compelling.
His use of Western art to illuminate this topic is particularly striking; it
is something to have a prophet to conduct you round an art gallery.
He has a grasp of the sweep of Christian history, and is alert to its
encouragements, its ambiguities and its contradictions, aware that historically the church has been both sign and counter-sign of the Kingdom
of God. He has vision that comprehends six continents and knowledge
and sympathy to understand their significance. And he has meditated
long on Scripture, and the insights he brings from that source enlighten
and refresh. This is indeed a book for those who want to know what
kind of day it is for the church, and how it differs from other days we
knew, or thought we knew. And it will also help the reader get out the

clothing required for such a day, and trouble any who decide to skulk at home instead.

Andrew F. Walls
Centre for the Study of Christianity in the Non-Western World
University of Edinburgh

Introduction

This book has been a long time in the making. In 1969 I sailed for Africa with my wife, Joyce, and our two small sons. That journey aboard a Nigerian cargo vessel was a defining moment in my life. For five weeks we made our way south, edging around the coast of West Africa, calling at ports in Senegal, Gambia, Liberia and Ghana, before finally moving up one of the lesser streams in the mighty Niger delta to a tiny port named Koko. That never-to-be-forgotten journey involved much more than moving through physical space; it was also a spiritual, intellectual and theological pilgrimage with results that were so far-reaching that I have often described them as like a 'second conversion'.

For more than a month at sea I talked with members of the Nigerian crew and with fellow passengers and as I did so many of my taken-for-granted assumptions concerning Africa, the world, and Christianity and its mission began to crumble. I vividly remember the ship's captain making a passionate protest at the manner in which rich Europeans were increasingly using his continent as their 'playground'. The chief radio officer politely suggested that my purpose in travelling to Nigeria was misguided since Africa's great need was not for 'more religion' (of which, he said, they had plenty already), but for an increase in science and technology. The themes of 'globalisation' and 'secularis-ation', both discussed in this book, were already present in these conversations.

Above all, though, that voyage and the subsequent experience of working with an African church in the rainforests of Eastern Nigeria, transformed my understanding of the Christian mission. Soon after our arrival I sat one Sunday morning on the veranda of the old mission house, listening with astonishment to the sound of beautiful Efik singing as songs of praise to God rose from dozens of congregations in the adjacent palm forests. Later, I was to discover that the church with which I served, one of the smaller Christian groupings in Nigeria, had close on a million members and rising. And then there were the questions asked by students, touching issues of critical importance to them, but matters which lay completely beyond the range of my inherited theology. This was Christianity, but not as I had known it, so that there were times when I felt like an alien visitor from another world. Slowly, as I reflected on these experiences, I came to realise how deeply my faith was conditioned by culture and how little I really understood the strange world of the Bible. And I began to wonder whether the designation 'missionary', which had been applied to me as I left my homeland, was not now a complete misnomer.

In recent years, as I have served as an advisor to a number of British missionary organisations, those memories have resurfaced during discussions of the crisis facing Protestant missionary work in a rapidly changing world. The culture-shock that I experienced in West Africa over thirty years ago has now become familiar to Western church and mission leaders as they struggle to make sense of a context in which their organisations look increasingly like boats stranded by a retreating tide. I attempt to describe and analyse this situation in Chapter 1 of this book, using the now familiar concept of 'paradigm change'. My aim in all that follows is to assist Western Christian leaders and thoughtful believers who (to use a biblical phrase) 'tremble for the ark of God', by tracing the historical roots of the crisis we face and suggesting precisely where the new frontiers of the Christian mission are located today. Then, having defined the problem, I seek to describe the challenges represented by secularisation (Chapter 2), pluralisation (Chapter 4) and globalisation (Chapter 6). Interwoven with these discussions are a series of chapters offering biblical reflection by means of a focus on selected texts which seem to speak with great relevance in relation to the frontiers I have identified. This use of the Bible signals my own belief in the authority of Scripture, but it also indicates a deep concern that the Bible must be allowed to speak to us today in ways that are fresh, dynamic and specifically relevant to the missionary challenges of the twenty-first century. I have attempted to engage in just such a process of listening afresh to the word of God, assisted by the biblical scholars whose work is cited in Chapters 3, 5 and 7.

One rather unusual feature of this book requires explanation, namely, my use of art to illustrate the argument. I am neither an historian of art nor an artist, so this is a rather risky business. However, I have come to appreciate, both as an individual and as a teacher, the enormous importance of the visual arts, both because of their ability to speak to us at a level that transcends rational discourse, and because of the manner in which paintings can illuminate the cultural and historical context within which we find ourselves. If any art historians should chance upon this book I beg their indulgence; at the same time, I will be gratified if readers find the masterpieces discussed here as enlightening, challenging and encouraging as I have done.

The list of people who have helped to bring this work to birth, and to whom I wish to express my gratitude, is considerable. My debts begin with my esteemed teacher, Professor Andrew Walls, whose influence can be detected on most of the pages that follow. I am grateful to him for both his teaching and example and for the generous Foreword he has written for this work. At an early stage of my writing I had the enormous privilege of discussing the issues raised here with Bishop Kenneth Cragg, whose remarkable 1968 book, *Christianity in World Perspective*, I had then recently discovered. I treasure the memory of those enriching conversations with one of the greatest missionary thinkers of the twentieth century. Dr David Cook, my colleague at the Whitefield Institute in Oxford, not only gave me great encouragement but made it possible for me to work in an environment which was wonderfully conducive for research and writing. I owe David, together with my colleagues John Lennox and Nigel Lee, my sincere thanks. At the same time, the work would probably never have been completed without the technical help of Ruth Robinson and Kate Dobson, who both responded to many cries for help when the computer crashed or a file was lost. In addition, I am grateful to many people who have either read part of the manuscript, or commented on material presented in lecture form: to the members of the Whitefield Institute postgraduate seminars in Oxford, the educationalists who attended the Stapleford Centre conference in 2001, and the scholars and ministers who commented on my Finlayson Lecture in Edinburgh in 2002, I am profoundly grateful. I also thank Howel Jones, Dr Jenny Taylor, Dr Andrew Smith, and my colleagues in the *Global Christian Library Project*, Pauline Hoggarth, Joe Kapoloyo, Robert Aboagye-Mensah, David Samuel and Peter Kuzmic, for their feedback and encouragement. This book would have been immensely poorer without the advice and criticism of this circle of colleagues and friends, although they are in no way responsible for the faults that remain.

One final word: I have already mentioned my wife, Joyce, in connection with our journey to Africa, and to her, above anyone else, my thanks are due, not simply for encouragement in this particular project, but for a shared pilgrimage during which her patience and love have been a blessing beyond words.

David Smith
Oxford, August 2002

1

The Challenges Facing the Missionary Movement

At the beginning of this third millennium the National Gallery in London mounted an exhibition of Christian art with the title 'Seeing Salvation'. In the introduction to the catalogue, the Director of the Gallery, Neil MacGregor, observed,

> All great collections of European painting are inevitably also great collections of Christian art. In the National Gallery, London, roughly one third of the pictures – and many of the finest – are of Christian subjects. This is hardly suprising, for after classical antiquity, Christianity has been the predominant force in shaping European cultures.
>
> (MacGregor: 2000, 6)

However, MacGregor immediately goes on to acknowledge that while a substantial proportion of the pictures in the collection are Christian, 'many of our visitors now are not'. A growing awareness of this fact provided the motivation for mounting the exhibition since MacGregor realised that thousands of visitors, whether tourists belonging to non-Christian religious traditions, or Europeans who are no longer biblically literate, view these great canvasses incomprehendingly and so focus their attention on the technical aspects of the art, rather than on the Christian *meaning* intended by the artists.

If the inability of many of the visitors to the National Gallery to recognise and interpret Christian symbols can be taken as evidence of the declining salience of the biblical story within the culture of the Western world, it is interesting to note that in the closing year of the twentieth century there was parallel evidence concerning the erosion of the other great metanarrative which has shaped the culture of modern Europe, namely, that of the Enlightenment. Writing in the

1

programme for the 1999 BBC Promenade Concerts, Michael Ignatieff pointed out that some of the great works to be performed during the season, including Beethoven's Choral Symphony and the 'Resurrection' Symphony of Gustav Mahler, could not be understood apart from 'the Enlightenment faith in human reason and endurance as the secular Providence of modern history'. However, living at the end of a dark century, Ignatieff said,

> ... we are no longer certain that we can believe such stories. There is enough barbarism close at hand to make us doubt that our species is marching together along a path toward civilisation. Indeed, in a Proms season of music devoted to the Ascent of Man ... *it is easy to feel that we are listening to the music of our lost hopes and illusions, reaching us like the last light from extinguished stars.*
>
> (Ignatieff: 1999, 8 [emphasis mine])

Taken together these two turn-of-the-century witnesses reflect very clearly the unmistakable 'sense of an ending' that pervades the culture of the Western world at the present time. Ignatieff's jeremiad serves to confirm the conviction held by many thoughtful Christians that the Enlightenment project was built on wholly inadequate foundations. The bells which ring out at the end of Mahler's magnificent symphony may suppress secular *angst* for a few hours but they cannot disguise the fragile basis of the hope they seek to express, the desperate longing to feel that one has not 'vainly lived and suffered'. Michael Ignatieff acknowledges that even this limited, secular affirmation has become difficult in our own time and he wonders how we can discover resources to continue 'this grand musical tradition of affirmation that seems to leave the language of praise all used up?' (*ibid.*: 10).

In a cultural context like this questions concerning the future of the Christian mission are unavoidable since, whatever the precise nature of the connection between the modern missionary movement and the Enlightenment, it is clear that the great age of Christian expansion, the period described by Kenneth Scott Latourette as the 'great century' in the history of the Christian mission, occurred at precisely the time that European economic and political power was being extended across the world. Indeed, when Andrew Walls analyses Christian history in terms of six successive eras in which the Christian faith has been trans-mitted across major cultural barriers, he describes the period which has witnessed the modern missionary movement as *the age of expanding Europe*. During this phase, he writes, 'The population of

Europe was exported to other continents and the dominance of Europe extended, until by the twentieth century people of European origin occupied, possessed, or dominated the greater part of the globe' (Walls: 1996, 21). Moreover, throughout most of this period Christianity was the professed religion of almost all European peoples, with the result that mission became inextricably linked with the expansion of Western influence and civilisation.

The title of this book, however, suggests that the linkage between mission and European civilisation must be traced back long before the dawn of the modern era since the basic presuppositions underlying this model of mission came to birth with the emergence of Christendom. The arrival of Columbus in the New World in 1492 was without doubt an event of enormous significance, but rather than marking the commencement of what we might call an 'imperial' model of mission, it merely represented the attempt to extend that model beyond the confines of Europe *where it had held sway for centuries*. The origins of the concept of a Christian empire, sometimes denoted by the phrase *Corpus Christianum*, are usually traced back to Constantine or Theodosius and the conversion of the emperor was clearly a watershed event in the history of the church. In the words of the Swiss theologian Walbert Buhlmann, 'Having Christianized the Roman Empire from within, having become a state religion, having received privileges and lands, the Jesus-movement... became an institution. The open city placed on a mountain (Matt. 5:14) became a fortress, with walls and moats' (Buhlmann: 1982, 67).

However, perhaps the crucial factor in the growth of a form of Christianity in which the profession of faith became bound up with the possession of territory is to be discovered during another great cultural transmission of the faith as vast numbers of Barbarian peoples from Northern Europe accepted Christian baptism (see Fletcher: 1997). The cultural and religious background of these peoples was significantly different from that of Rome or Greece in that their traditional, primal religions made it impossible for them to distinguish the realms of the sacred and the secular. Thus was born the concept of a people united by a single body of belief and of Christianity as a territorial religion. From such obscure beginnings, Christendom grew and developed over a very long period of time to become a religious ideology which has proved amazingly resilient. While the Reformation led to the fragmentation of Christendom it retained many of its fundamental assumptions so that the *spirit* of Christendom has persisted across the centuries,

3

reflected in phrases and slogans which still remain in use today to describe the task of evangelism and mission. Thus, when Western Christians deplore the refusal of public institutions to identify Christ with Christmas, or when Jehovah's Witnesses are treated with contempt or disdain, or even when evangelists in Northern Nigeria enter Muslim areas to announce a forthcoming 'Crusade', we realise that the shadow cast by Christendom is both long and undimmed.

Nonetheless, it is quite clear by now that this particular model of the Christian mission has lost its credibility and cannot survive. In fact, the erosion of the Christendom concept commenced as soon as the attempt was made to transmit the faith beyond the confines of its European heartlands. Thus, from the sixteenth century onwards, and with ever-increasing momentum during the period Latourette called the 'great century', a form of Christianity thoroughly acculturated within Europe 'had to extend its consciousness, its vision, and eventually its theology, to cope with the realities of the world beyond Europe' (Walls: 1995, 2). Christendom's division of the world and its peoples into two great blocs – *here* a culture shaped by the Gospel; *there* a realm of ignorance and darkness (a categorisation that continued to inform the Western mind in various secularised reworkings) – has increasingly seemed to be implausible and unbelievable. In Buhlmann's words, 'Until recently the world was divided in two: the church and the missions . . . The church was the centre, the missions were its periphery. We had the model over here, the copy over there.' This schema will no longer work, he says, since we have witnessed a historic shift in which the 'centre of gravity' of the Christian movement has now been transferred to the southern hemisphere (Buhlmann: 1982, 247). Meantime, the barbarism which has all too frequently disfigured the culture of Europe, combined with the steady and accelerating recession in the influence of Christianity in its traditional heartlands, makes it impossible to continue to claim that European civilisation remains a 'Christian culture'.

Clearly, in a context like this, many questions arise concerning the future of Christian mission. Let me pose some of them in rather stark language. Does not missionary talk of the *conquest* of the world sound extremely discordant and offensive in an age when people have become rightly suspicious of such terminology? Can we continue to talk of the *future* of mission in the language of the past, as though the world in which it must be done has not changed? And, given a culture in which institutional Christianity seems to be facing a supreme crisis and even the rumours of God are fading, where will we find the *resources* in personnel and funding to continue the kind of global enterprise we have associated with cross-cultural mission? These questions become urgent in the light of the findings of Wilbert Shenk that the study of the missionary movement since the 1920s leaves the impression that 'an ageing movement, increasingly unable to adapt to the times' has found its basic structures and assumptions rendered irrelevant and that 'with the end of the modern period in world history has also come the end of modern missions' (Shenk: 1999, 165).

In a situation like this serious biblical and theological reflection on the future of the Christian mission becomes an urgent priority. Indeed, just such reflection has been under way for some time now, boosted by the *magnum opus* of the late David Bosch, *Transforming Mission*. In this influential book Bosch attempted to describe what he called the 'Emerging Ecumenical Missionary Paradigm'. He acknowledged that we are living through a time of deep uncertainty and confusion not unlike previous periods in the history of mission when Christians have faced major change in the church and in the world. Bosch observed that such transitions are always difficult to negotiate:

> New paradigms do not establish themselves overnight. They take decades, even centuries, to develop distinctive contours. The new paradigm is therefore still emerging and it is, as yet, not clear which shape it will eventually adopt. For the most part we are, at the moment, thinking and working in terms of *two* paradigms. (Bosch: 1991, 349)

In the light of this comment I want to devote the remainder of this chapter to a consideration of the actual or possible responses to this situation. How *are* Christians reacting to the current crisis in mission? Is it possible to begin to discern the contours of an emerging model of mission and, if so, what are its leading features?

Crisis! What Crisis?

The first position I want to describe can be called the *business as usual* response. This reaction is found among Christians who have come to identify mission with one particular, passing paradigm. The conditional nature of any and all of our understandings of the missionary calling of the people of God is overlooked and one local expression of missionary obedience and practice is elevated to the status of an unchanging absolute and invested with all the authority of divine revelation. To abandon *this* position, it is argued, is to renege on the call of Christ to obey the 'great commission'. To other people it seems obvious that the particular model being defended is creaking at the seams, yet those who cling to it cannot face the prospect of its demise and so live in a condition of denial.

I suggest that this response is widespread among Evangelicals and can be detected in a great deal of missionary literature. For example, the seemingly unending series of programmes and strategies for world evangelisation which were promoted in the approach to the year AD 2000 had in common a steadfast denial of the realities of Western secularisation, combined with an approach to the non-Western world which was, at best, paternalistic, at worst, neo-colonial. Thus, the founder of the DAWN project (DAWN stands for 'Discipling A Whole Nation') claimed that this movement, which offers techniques designed to lead directly to the completion of the great commission and the end of the world, had swept across England, enthusiastically endorsed by the leaders of all denominations, including the then Archbishop of Canterbury. The Church of England was said to have been a staid and static church in terrible decline before the adoption of DAWN strategies, but was revived and planting a new congregation every week. The upshot of all this was, according to the writer, that God was 'anointing the Church in England to *get back to its historic role* as one of the leading missionary sending nations in the world' (Montgomery: 1997, 54 [emphasis mine]). Any doubt that such sentiments amounted to a desire to turn the clock back are banished when we read that the Church in England could 'return to its former colonies' and pioneer a new strategy in missions (*ibid.*).

It is difficult to know whether to treat such descriptions as simply naïve wishful thinking or wilful blindness, but whatever the explanation, we are clearly dealing with an approach that ignores both the challenge of mission in the modern West and renders invisible the emergence of what Buhlmann has called 'the Third Church' in the non-Western world. Missiology of this kind involves an irresponsible flight from reality and a refusal to face the real challenge of discovering the true frontiers of Christian mission in the third millennium.

However, it is important to notice that while the position just described may appear anachronistic, it is attractive to many Christians who find themselves confused and bewildered by the tensions and contradictions that exist in a time of transition. It is not easy to live between paradigms at a point when the old model no longer works and the new one has not yet emerged. A strategy of mission that assures anxious Christians that nothing has really changed, that Christian conquest of the world remains assured, and that with one final push we can actually precipitate the end of all things and the return of the Lord, obviously has power to reassure the troubled. Thus, when a highly respected missionary strategist writes that the 'tide of the gospel has risen and flowed over two thirds of the earth, and is lapping at the one third where the final bastions and citadels of Satan's kingdom have yet to be broken down' (Johnstone: 1998, 215–16), it is tempting to accept such an analysis since it confirms that nothing has really changed in the world and the inherited paradigm of mission can be retained. Sadly, analyses of this kind rest upon nineteenth-century assumptions which involve the presupposition that the contemporary West is an area *immersed* in the Gospel tide, while peoples in the so-called 10/40 window are under satanic domination to a degree found nowhere else on the planet. The cities of Accra, Delhi and Beijing are thus classified as 'citadels of Satan'; London, Berlin, even Las Vegas, are not viewed as legitimate missionary territory since they are located in areas that have been 'evangelised'. Whatever else may be said about such an approach, it is difficult to see how it connects with the real world we know from daily experience at the beginning of the twenty-first century.

These comments are certainly not meant to impugn the integrity or sincerity of Christians who continue to operate within a fading missionary paradigm. Indeed, such people often reveal a concern for God's glory and a deep compassion for the world that would put many of us to shame and in these and many other ways their commitment demands imitation rather than rejection. Nonetheless, precisely *because* we share such a concern for the glory of God in a rapidly changing world, we are bound to engage in a search for a new paradigm of faithful, missionary obedience in the third millennium. There is an urgent need to break out from a situation in which the relics of the lost paradigm 'hold us hostage to the past and make it difficult to create a new paradigm' (Mead: 1988, 18). Meantime, as Loren Mead observes, many people react in this context with denial, depression and *anger*: 'I see it in the way people at all levels engage in civil wars or try to purge one another for one reason or another' (*ibid.*: 62). This alerts us to the fact that the time between paradigms is likely to witness increased stress within the Body of Christ and is a situation in which there is need for greater vigilance than ever if we are to maintain the unity of the people of God.

Back to Basics

The second position I want to notice can be called that of the *radical revisionists*. As long ago as 1951 Max Warren noted that we were living through the end of an age and that in both East and West 'the old landmarks are disappearing'. Warren commented,

> In this testing situation it is essential that the particular form of the missionary enterprise shall be scrutinized afresh to see what, if any, are the elements of its past organization that can with advantage be carried over into the future . . . Beyond this it is surely necessary to go even further and to ask the direct question – '*Have we reached the end of the missionary age in any shape recognizably continuous with the past?*' (Warren: 1951, 103 [emphasis mine])

In the middle of the twentieth century Warren had sensed that the changes taking place in the world were of such a profound and far-reaching nature that no mere tinkering with the structures of mission would suffice and he anticipated what we have come to know as a paradigm shift in the Christian mission. At the beginning of the third millennium it has become clear to many thoughtful observers that we have indeed reached the end of the era of modern missions and a growing chorus of voices can now be heard demanding a radically new approach. For example, the Canadian theologian Douglas John Hall wrote a book with the title *Christian Mission: The Stewardship of Life in the Kingdom of Death* in which he sought to articulate 'a new under-standing of our mission' that relates Christian witness to the realities of a culture in which powerful nations have entered into a covenant with death. Hall described the inherited model of mission as one that was fatally flawed by the concept of 'conquering for Christ' and he proposed a root-and-branch rejection of this imagery. The question of Jesus, 'What does it profit one to gain the whole world and lose one's soul?' could be applied to the church: what if the church gained the world, in the manner intended by the church-growth missiologists, and, in the process, lost its soul? The equating of missionary success with the expansion of the church subverts a basic principle of the Gospel since, Hall said, 'By such logic, Jesus' own mission must be regarded as a failure . . . But perhaps the logic of the cross must call into question the whole assumption that faithfulness to the mission means the expansion of the missionary community' (Hall: 1985, 18).

Douglas John Hall believes that the new paradigm of mission he is advocating would involve a *return* to an apostolic model of the church in which a 'disciple community' loses itself in the service of the world and bears costly and prophetic witness to the God of life in a world in thrall to the idols of death. In Hall's words,

> In the kingdom God is building in the midst of death's kingdom, system-atic theology will not be queen, and the church will not be a great property-holding multinational, and Christian armies will not go off to glorious death . . . All that . . . will exist for the church of the future only as the record of a bad temptation, rejected by Jesus and picked up by his church, which finally achieved little if anything of true significance thereby. (Hall: 1985, 19)

There is much to be learned from works like this and it is impossible not to admire Hall's attempt to articulate a fresh vision for the Christian mission. His analysis of Western culture in the light of Isaiah 28:14–22, in which the nations refuse the God of life and enter into a covenant with death, is compelling. Moreover, he shows great courage in suggesting that 'many of the earth's billions today' regard North America as the source of the world's sickness and that this favoured continent may prove to be the vulnerable channel 'through which Sheol could one day spew its lava over the face of the green planet' (*ibid.*: 35). In other words, far from being a region immersed in the truth of the gospel, *the Western world constitutes one of the supreme missionary challenges of this, or any other, age.*

However, there are dangers in this type of *revisionism* since it is possible that it leads beyond merely abandoning an outdated model of mission, to the loss of fundamental aspects of mission itself. It is, in other words, at the opposite end of the spectrum to the *conservationist* tactic discussed earlier. Hall's depiction of the received paradigm of mission as one characterised above all else by the motif of the *conquest* of the world in the name of Christ does scant justice to the records of humble and sacrificial service which fill the annals of missionary history. If after the holocaust, the entire heritage of cross-cultural missionary service must be repudiated (as Hall seems to suggest), what then happens to the coherence of the Christian movement across the ages? It simply will not do to brand the entire effort with the charges laid against *conquistadores* and imperialists when the historical record reveals a far more nuanced picture. And while Hall's proposal that mission should in the future be focused on 'the stewardship of life in the kingdom of death' merits careful consideration, we are bound to

9

ask why he is so reticent about inviting people to *turn* from death and to *receive* the gift of life.

I am reminded here of the experience of the Gambian Christian convert from Islam, Lamin Sanneh. In an article entitled 'Christian Missions and the Western Guilt Complex', Sanneh recalls that when at the age of eighteen he approached an English Methodist missionary with a request to be baptised, he was invited to reconsider his decision! In this liberal Methodist tradition, he says, 'I first encountered the guilt complex about missions which I have since come to know so well after living for more than two decades in the West' (Sanneh: 1987, 330). Yet, as Sanneh points out, the stigmatising of the missionary movement as the religious agent of colonialism ignores the empirical fact that colonial power was 'irreparably damaged by the consequences of vernacular translation – and often by other activities of the missionaries' (*ibid*.: 331). In other words, modern missions, whatever their failings and shortcomings, formed the agency by means of which indigenous languages and local cultures were preserved and non-Western peoples were equipped with a transcendent source of authority which enabled them to critique racism and imperialism and recover their own sense of worth and value.

So then, if neither the conservative *business as usual* response nor the *radical revisionist* approach to the present crisis in mission are adequate, what path should we take as we seek for a new model of the Christian mission? I propose to explore precisely this question in the remainder of this book and to do so in terms of what Wilbert Shenk has characterised as *a search for the new frontiers of mission*. Shenk comments helpfully,

> It is in the nature of mission always to seek the frontier where the struggle between faith and unfaith is most clearly and urgently drawn. The first essential of leadership, the one above all others with regard to mission, is to see the vision of the reign of God being established in these frontier situations and then to hold that before the church. All else is secondary. (Shenk: 1999, 183)

Most of the frustrations and dilemmas facing traditional missionary organisations and their supporters today arise from the fact that modern mission agencies came into existence in order to facilitate mission at frontiers far away in Africa, Asia and Latin America. The institutions and structures of mission designed to operate at these frontiers have remained in place at a time when the geographical, cultural and social location of mission has moved elsewhere. Not surprisingly, the traditional language used to report missionary activity often seems hollow and unreal. As Shenk puts it, *missions are today in search of mission*; agencies and institutions that once did pioneering work at the cutting edges of the Christian mission have too often been left facing in the wrong direction as the battle has moved on. In this situation they face a stark choice: either they engage in a radical re-formation, repositioning themselves to respond to the quite new challenges of the twenty-first century, or they are doomed to rapid and rather sad decline and extinction. A recent study of the crisis facing North American mission agencies concludes that unless they can break away from their essentially nineteenth-century, culturally modernist mindset and embrace the new opportunities presented in the postmodern age, they will soon be known only to historians. Indeed, missions have need of penitence since they 'have infected a world church with the disease of modernity'. As a result, traditional agencies may be in danger of 'being judged unworthy to carry the mantle God once placed on North American missions' (Engel and Dyrness: 2000, 78).

In the chapters that follow I wish to engage in a search for the new frontiers of mission today and to discuss the changes that will be required, mentally, structurally and theologically, if the church is to obey Christ in relevant and faithful witness in this new context.

I want to end this chapter where it began, in the National Gallery in London. Interestingly, although the 'Seeing Salvation' exhibition was prompted by the awareness of increasing biblical illiteracy, the final room bore the title 'The Abiding Presence'. It contained a series of modern images of Christ, including famous canvasses by Holman Hunt and Salvador Dali and the sketches for the great tapestry of Christ in glory by Graham Sutherland which hangs in Coventry Cathedral. It also included a huge canvas of Stanley Spencer's in which Christ is depicted carrying his cross through the artist's native village of Cookham in Berkshire (picture 1). This painting was completed in 1920 when memories of the Great War were still fresh in people's minds. That terrible conflict, hints of which are to be seen in Spencer's painting, shattered both the belief that European culture was in some sense 'Christian' *and* the confidence of those who had trusted the process of evolution to ensure the continuing 'ascent of man'. In this situation, Spencer depicts a Christ who transforms a dark and despairing world and gives hope and meaning to people in his village, including the most humble of folk. Spencer said that he had come to realise that the cross of Jesus

11

made everything holy: 'The instinct of Moses to take his shoes off when he saw the burning bush was similar to my feelings. I saw many burning bushes in Cookham.' Perhaps one aspect of the emerging paradigm of mission will involve the discovery of burning bushes in unlikely places in our postmodern culture and the humble and grateful acknowledgement of the prevenient grace of God which has always preceded the arrival of the ambassadors of Christ at every new frontier of mission.

2

Finding the New Frontiers:
(1) The Challenge of Secularisation

In 1533 the artist Hans Holbein completed a huge painting with the title *The Ambassadors* (picture 2). This great work, which now hangs with many of the pictures mentioned in the previous chapter in the National Gallery, London, has been the subject of endless debate. It depicts two French visitors to the court of Henry VIII standing either side of a double-level table which is laden with a variety of objects representing the new world of humanist learning. The items at the centre of the picture, including both terrestrial and celestial globes, are related to the emerging sciences of astronomy, geometry and mathematics and to the arts of music and literature. Together they celebrate Renaissance scholarship and anticipate the social and cultural revolution which would result from this new learning.

However, celebration is tempered by a profound sense of unease generated by the awareness that the undoubted progress stemming from this explosion of knowledge would be likely to exact a considerable psychological, social and spiritual price. The painting is 'a testament by Holbein and his patron to their shared concerns in the uncertain England of 1533' (Wilson: 1997, 197). It is littered with inconsistencies and enigmas: the lute has a broken string, on the celestial globe a hen attacks a bird of prey, and there is something deeply worrying about the men themselves as they stare directly at us, emotionless, expressionless and pale. At the top left-hand corner of the picture, half concealed behind the intimidating curtain that forms the backcloth to the scene, is a crucifix. As the new learning takes centre stage and human knowledge of the world increases exponentially, Holbein seems to be saying, so the message of Christ crucified will be driven to the margins of culture and society. In other words, the picture anticipates precisely the process of *secularisation.*

Even more worrying is the strange, distorted skull which the artist has placed like some great tear in the canvas at the feet of the ambassadors. Skulls were a common enough feature of medieval art and acted as a *memento mori,* a reminder of death. There is no doubt that this is Holbein's intention, but in this case the message seems to be yet more specific and powerful: if in the revolutionary times ahead, Christ and the message of the cross are displaced as human achievement leads people to conclude that divine grace is redundant, how then will men like these proud and wealthy ambassadors be able to cope with death? What kind of world will it be in which humanist knowledge enables people to extend their control over the world, yet at the same time agreement concerning the *meaning* of existence is eroded? The message of *The Ambassadors* implies that the ability to plot the motion of the stars will not help a man find direction in his own life, nor will the sweet sound of the lute soothe his nerves 'once the whiff of a corpse has penetrated his nostrils'. Indeed, the greatest of all humanist institutions, the university, 'is a mausoleum of dead ideas' once faith has been lost and 'the ultimate necessity is Death' (Carroll: 1993, 32).

Clearly, Hans Holbein lived through a period when changes of absolutely fundamental importance were occurring within European culture. When he was a boy of fifteen, the fiery preaching of Savanarola rocked the city of Florence, anticipating by two decades the later demands of Martin Luther. Holbein was himself deeply influenced by the Reformation, and yet, like Erasmus (whose portrait he painted many times), he was fearful that the changes occuring around him could too easily run out of control and result in the complete fragmentation of Western society and culture. In 1526 he arrived in London just as copies of Tyndale's translation of the New Testament were being smuggled across the Channel and distributed illicitly in England. Indeed, *The Ambassadors* was painted in the eye of the storm of the English Reformation. Holbein thus lived through an era of unprecedented change in the way people thought about art, religion, science, politics and society and he 'could not be indifferent to the issues which were tearing jagged holes in the fabric of Christian Europe' (Wilson: 1997, 2).

In order to see these events in a wider context, it is important to recall that, three years before Holbein's birth, Columbus had landed in the 'New World'. Whatever else may be said about this event, it marked the beginning of the first major cycle of Western missionary activity beyond Christendom. This expansion of Europe, with its inter-locking religious, political and economic motivation, was to have an enormous impact upon the history of the world and the identification of Christianity with the *conquistadores* has rightly been said to rest upon an 'imperial missiology'. Nonetheless, a recent study of this period which records in great detail the most sordid aspects of the European encounter with primal peoples contains generous acknowledgement of the positive contribution of missionaries during this first great venture beyond the European heartland of the faith:

> The European faith eventually became for tribal peoples worldwide both an important solace against, and a social bridge into, the alien world of their colonisers. Moreover, the army of genuinely humane missionaries who travelled out to the colonies to evangelise *often served as important political champions for their indigenous flock.*
>
> (Cocker: 1999, 15 [emphasis mine])

There is a further point, however, in that this cross-cultural movement was, in the course of time, to open channels of knowledge and com-munication which would challenge European assumptions and liberate Christianity from its identification with the culture of the Western world. This was, of course, an unintended consequence of the expansion of European power and influence, which occurred at precisely the point at which the triumph of Christianity within the West had seemed assured. The last surviving pagan peoples within Europe had received Christian baptism, Islam had been expelled from the Iberian peninsula, and the agenda of medieval theology seemed to have been completed. As the fifteenth century drew to a close, few could have anticipated that the coming encounter with non-Western peoples would eventually shatter the medieval picture of the terrestrial globe as surely as the discoveries of a Polish astronomer in the year of Holbein's death were destined to undermine its assumptions concerning the cosmos.

Thus, the significance of this period so far as the Christian mission is concerned is related to two factors. First, the discovery of peoples and cultures outside Christendom, and the gradual realisation that these alternative world-views posed previously unheard of questions for theology, was deeply challenging for a church so long conditioned by the thought and culture of Europe. In the course of the following centuries European Christians were required to expand their understanding and their vision in order to cope with the new experience of a wider world which simply could not be accommodated within the previous framework of philosophical and theological knowledge – a task which is, indeed, still ongoing. In other words, Christendom began the centuries-long process of coming to terms with the realities of *cultural and religious pluralism.*

The implications of pluralisation for the Christian mission will concern us in a later chapter. Here we will consider the second factor which emerges within this period and now constitutes a major challenge to mission in the twenty-first century, namely the beginnings of *secularisation* in Europe.

The Dawn of the Modern World

The premonitions of disaster felt by Holbein, and reflected so remarkably in his art, were more than fulfilled in the course of the next century. The Reformation led to the religious and political division of Europe as Christendom splintered into warring states denominated by different theological confessions. While Luther and Calvin challenged the Pope's view of the Gospel, they did not question the basic structures of the *Corpus Christianum* regarding the relationship between religion and territory and the need for the state to enforce religious conformity. The inevitable and tragic result of the magisterial Reformation was that Europe became a religious battlefield. Germany, France, the Netherlands, England, Scotland and Ireland all witnessed bloodshed on a massive scale as attempts were made by Catholics, Lutherans and Calvinists to impose sectarian confessions of faith on the emerging nations of Europe. Historians like Theodore Rabb have argued that these confessional wars, and especially the Thirty Years War in Germany, mark a key turning point in the history of Europe as a whole. By the end of this period the assumption that unity of religious belief was a necessary basis for common life (a view that had been an unquestioned axiom within Christendom) was increasingly replaced by the conviction that *religious passion destroys social peace* (Pannenberg: 1988, 12). The cross of Christ, brandished in the defence of narrow nationalisms and held before armies of Christians 'marching as to war', was now quietly moved to the edge of the picture by a new breed of intellectuals determined to forge a more rational and humane way forward.

Take, for example, René Descartes. Almost exactly one hundred years after Holbein finished work on *The Ambassadors* the young Descartes was returning from Germany where he had been engaged in war service. On his way home the onset of winter forced him to take shelter and, he tells us, 'I spent the whole day shut up in a room heated by an enclosed stove, where I had complete leisure to meditate on my own thoughts' (Descartes 1968: 35). It is reasonable to suppose that the thoughts preoccupying the brilliant mind of this young Frenchman concerned the chaotic condition of Christendom. How was one to discover a way beyond the violence spawned by rival dogmatisms? Certainly, the meditations that resulted from his enforced isolation changed the course of Western intellectual history. The way forward, he concludes, is to subject everything to reason; clear the decks of all received knowledge, challenge all authorities, and search for what is certain, even if this leads to the conclusion 'that there is nothing certain in the world' (*ibid.*: 102). Not only is the cross being moved from the centre of the world-picture, *the real threat of meaninglessness represented by Holbein's distorted skull now comes into view.*

Indeed, for one of Descartes' best-known contemporaries this was precisely the issue that was at stake as individuals struggled to discover firm ground beneath their feet when all the foundations seemed to be collapsing. Blaise Pascal was, like Descartes, a thoroughly modern man, aware of the failings and inadequacies of traditional philosophical and theological formulations and deeply committed to scientific enquiry. Yet Pascal was also profoundly conscious of the deepening spiritual crisis of the age and the growing incidence of boredom, or *anomie*, in the experience of people whose ceaseless activity failed to conceal their sense of alienation and loneliness. In words that seem to confirm the accuracy of Holbein's almost prophetic insights, Pascal observed: 'Being unable to cure death, wretchedness and ignorance, men have decided, in order to be happy, not to think about such things' (Pascal: 1966, 66). Modern people, Pascal observed, were terrified of being left alone and seemed unable to cope with solitude and silence: 'If our condition were truly happy we should not need to divert ourselves from thinking about it' (*ibid.*: 48). In language which anticipates much later analyses of the dilemmas facing people in a world which has made man 'the measure of all things', Pascal describes his contemporaries as 'floating in a medium of vast extent, always drifting uncertainly, blown to and fro'. Nothing stands still for us, he says,

> We burn with desire to find a firm footing, an ultimate, lasting base on which to build a tower rising up to infinity, but our whole foundation cracks and the earth opens up into the depths of the abyss. (*ibid.*: 92)

While Pascal understood perfectly well the reaction against the medieval world-view and the challenge to traditional religious authorities, he also believed that the rationalist approach taken by Descartes was a path which would lead humankind ever nearer to the edge of this yawning abyss. To propose rational thought as the basis of *all* human knowledge was to offer a cure for the ills of the age which would, in time, prove infinitely worse than the disease. Reason must recognise that 'there are an infinite number of things which are beyond it. It is merely feeble if it does not go as far as to recognize that' (*ibid.*: 85).

Blaise Pascal was at one and the same time a scientific pioneer whose inventions anticipated modern computers and public transport systems, a Christian apologist of rare sensitivity and insight in the context of early modernity, and an important precursor of existentialist philosophy. Yet, however he might disagree with Descartes on the priority of human reason, the debate between them occurred *within the framework of European modernity.* For Pascal, as much as for Descartes, the scientific revolution has transformed the world forever and there can be no way of recovering the 'sacred canopy' which once extended its reach over all aspects of human life. The new cosmology has won the day and opened up vistas revealing the unimaginable immensity of space. Pascal confesses that the Copernican revolution leaves him awed and stunned:

> When I consider the brief span of my life absorbed into the eternity which comes before and after – *as the remembrance of a guest that tarrieth but a day* – the small space I occupy and which I see swallowed up in the infinite spaces of which I know nothing and which know nothing of me, I take fright and am amazed to see myself here rather than there, now rather than then. Who put me here? By whose command and act were this time and place allotted to me? (*ibid.*: 48)

The point here is that the new knowledge made possible by the instruments on the table at the centre of Holbein's painting has created a situation in which faith involves a struggle, or, as Pascal puts it, a *gamble.* It has lost its axiomatic, taken-for-granted quality and is in the process of becoming a matter of personal choice and decision. Indeed, for all the differences between them, what binds Columbus, Luther, Galileo, Descartes and Pascal together and defines them as *modern* people, is that, to a greater or lesser degree, they moved beyond the medieval world-view and 'gave priority to their own experience, their own self-determination, in the discovery of a new reality' (Ambler: 1999, 137).

Mission and the Enlightenment

René Descartes and Blaise Pascal can be regarded as two representative, or paradigmatic, figures at the dawn of European modernity. Pascal articulated a *religious* response to the new world being opened up by humanist learning, a response which was to be echoed later in the emergence of the pietists in Germany and in various movements of revival throughout Europe in the eighteenth and nineteenth centuries. In his insistence on the personal nature of religious experience and the distancing of the believer's knowledge of God from the epistemological discussions of the philosophers and scholars, Pascal charted a way forward for Christians in the modern West and provided a kind of template for religion in the context of modernity. The problem, however, was that, in the long run, this was to lead to the *privatisation* of faith as the religious realm was increasingly sealed off from matters of fact and knowledge to which those in the Cartesian tradition claimed exclusive access. The importance of this in relation to mission, as we shall see, is that the Christianity which was to be taken around the world through the agency of the missionary movement was itself shaped in significant ways by the secularisation of the West, a fact that created difficulties and tensions at the point of encounter with both *pre-modern* cultures and with peoples schooled by other religious traditions, notably in this respect, Islam.

As Pascal feared, the humanist stress on the priority of reason created a context in which traditional sources of wisdom and knowledge became increasingly suspect. Once it became accepted that the essential nature of human beings was to be identified with their rationality, then the unquestioned axioms of the medieval world were bound to be abandoned and traditional religious categories of knowledge, such as revelation and ancient tradition, were challenged. Such ideas led to the Enlightenment, which 'pushed the self-affirmation of modernity even further, dispensing finally with all reference to the Other as a source of truth or value' (Ambler: 1999, 142). There is a movement here from secularisation, understood as a cultural change that was not intrinsically hostile to religion, toward *secularism*. Thus, by the nineteenth century almost all of those who claimed to be working for the liberation of humankind were rationalists, if not materialists. Later modernity thus involved the assertion of the autonomy of human beings and the attempt to gain control over nature and society, 'first by understanding them analytically, then by manipulating them technologically and organisationally' (*ibid.*).

At precisely the point at which the impact of the Enlightenment was being felt throughout Europe, the second great cycle of Christian mission beyond Christendom began. Whereas, as we have seen, the first cycle had been associated with the expansionism of the Iberian powers and was Roman Catholic in character, the second occurred in conjunction with the spread of British influence around the world in the wake of the industrial revolution and was Protestant and Evangelical in form. David Bosch claims that the entire modern missionary movement was, at one level, a child of the Enlightenment:

> It was, after all, the new expansionist worldview which pushed Europe's horizons beyond the Mediterranean Sea and the Atlantic Ocean and thus paved the way for the world-wide Christian missionary outreach. (Bosch: 1991, 274)

It is important to stress that this second cycle of mission, no less than the first, involved the preaching of the Christian message beyond Christendom. Despite the obvious differences between the Roman Catholic missionaries who accompanied the *conquistadores* in the sixteenth century and the Protestants who were to follow British explorers and traders three hundred years later, both operated with a model of the world that assumed the fundamentally Christian character of the West. For William Carey, no less than for Francis Xavier or Matteo Ricci, mission involved a movement *from* the West *to* those regions of the world where Christ remained unknown, which had been brought to the consciousness of Europeans through the 'Age of Discovery'. Consequently, the missionary societies which came into being at this time were designed to facilitate the spread of the Christian faith beyond Christendom. By contrast, the revival movement which had swept through Britain and North America in the eighteenth century was described as the 'Great Awakening', terminology which clearly implied the renewal and recovery of something previously known and experienced.

In the course of the nineteenth century the enormous growth of the Evangelical movement in Britain and the United States and the expansion of Western economic and political power across the world had the effect of hardening the distinction between 'evangelism' – as an activity designed to make nominal Western Christians into real believers – and 'mission' – as the form of witness required overseas among primitive peoples lacking the blessings of a Christian civilisation. Tragically, few Christians at the time seemed to realise that the driving force in Western culture was less and less to be found in beliefs based upon the Bible, but was provided by philosophers and writers who understood their task in Promethean terms as being one of measuring and transforming the world on the basis of human reason. Thus, in 1795, at the very point at which the Protestant missionary movement was being launched, the Marquis de Condorcet published his *Sketch for a Historical Picture of the Progress of the Human Mind*, a hugely influential book which articulated with great clarity the Enlightenment faith in the perfectibility of humankind and the certainty of its progress toward an age of unprecedented prosperity and happiness. For Condorcet, paradise was not something that had been lost, rather it lies in the future as Western man fulfills his destiny, using the power of unfettered reason to chart the course toward utopia (Goudzwaard: 1997, 40). Within a quarter of a century, this belief in the inevitable progress of the human race had become axiomatic among many Western intellectuals, a fact reflected in the inscription placed by an admiring student on the tomb of the French utopian socialist, Saint-Simon: 'The golden age does not lie behind us, but ahead of us.'

Once again, the most perceptive critique of these cultural trends was to come from the brush of an artist rather than the pen of a theologian. In the year that Condorcet's work appeared, William Blake produced two pictures, one depicting Isaac Newton (picture 3), the other a representation of the ancient Babylonian king, Nebuchadnezzar (picture 4). Newton is drawn naked, bending over a pair of compasses with which he is characteristically measuring some aspect of nature. His body is that of an ideal man, without blemish and physically powerful, a perfect hero-figure befitting of the darling of the Enlightenment. However, Blake suggests that the scientist's obsession with measurement, his conviction that everything in the cosmos can be calculated and understood by the power of reason, is resulting in a dangerous reduction of the understanding of reality as things that are vital to a true human existence are lost. Indeed, if modern man allows himself to be seduced by the emerging secular gospel of Progress, he will end up not in paradise, but in the madhouse.

Thus, in the second picture, Nebuchadnezzar crawls on all fours like a wild beast, his face wearing a vacant stare, which indicates that his mind, *his reason*, has gone. If man is regarded as nothing more than a 'thinking being', Blake seems to imply, then he runs the risk of the loss of reason and will end up living an utterly meaningless and hopeless existence. The allusion here is obviously to the biblical story in the book of Daniel in which, as a consequence of his inordinate pride in his own achievements, Nebuchadnezzar is driven from his throne and lives as a beast in the field. Blake traces an exact parallel between the biblical narrative and the hubris of the Enlightenment and warns that the path being followed by intellectuals in the late eighteenth century will lead, not to universal happiness, but to insanity, humiliation and misery.

Although William Blake was not an Evangelical Christian, there is an interesting overlap between his radical critique of the Enlightenment and the beginnings of Protestant missions. William Carey's famous *Enquiry into the Obligations of Christians to use Means for the Conversion of the Heathen* was published in 1792 by the London printer Joseph Johnson, on whose press Tom Paine's *The Rights of Man* and Mary Wollstonecraft's *Vindication of the Rights of Women* were also printed. Indeed, it was in Johnson's house that Blake is reported to have warned Paine of the dangers posed by the repressive actions of a conservative government, urging him to flee to Paris. While Carey and his colleagues rejected Paine's rationalism, this overlapping of two worlds reminds us that Baptist missionaries in the 1790s came from a dissenting tradition which shaped their understanding of the Gospel in ways that meant that they shared some of the insights of William Blake. Like him, they abhorred religious tyranny and denounced a hierarchical social system which sanctified inherited privilege and power while discriminating against the poor. And it is worth pointing out that if Blake lived his life 'on the edge of subsistence' (Rowland: 2000, 13) and possessed an extraordinary insight into the importance of the voices of people from the margins, Carey and his co-workers established something close to a Christian commune in India in which membership was restricted to people willing to renounce the right to private property and to abstain from seeking personal gain through commercial activities. In common with many of the earliest Evangelicals, Carey and his friends saw no necessary conflict between their faith in Christ and the humanitarianism of the new age.

Mission and the Age of Empire

In the course of the nineteenth century the split between the realm of facts, established by means of scientific investigation, and mere opinions or beliefs widened. Perhaps the most significant change in this respect relates to the emergence of economics as a science and the uncoupling of the pursuit of wealth and the practice of business from normative ethical principles derived from the Bible. In the medieval world it was taken for granted that the economic arena required ethical and theological regulation. Adam Smith, the father of the modern science of economics, inherited an essentially deistic religion which banished God to the margins of history and the cosmos, allowing him only walk-on parts in the modern drama when the main actors needed a breather or forgot their lines. As the brilliant work of Isaac Newton had opened up the physical world to human understanding and manipulation, so the social and economic realms were now seen to be open to investigation and the discovery of the laws operating within them. Inherited theological principles were regarded as barriers to suc-cessful economic activity, to be cast aside in order that society might prosper and grow in line with the natural laws built into the fabric of things. The pursuit of wealth was thus removed from the controls derived from transcendent moral values and was *secularised.* God's place in the new scheme of things no longer guaranteed certain restraints upon human greed and avarice, but rather involved an in-visible and mysterious role which ensured that the newly released economic drive of modern entrepreneurs and capitalists would, in the long run, work for the common good. There was, Adam Smith believed, an 'invisible hand' which would ensure that the severing of economic life from traditional ethical restraints would not result in social chaos, since the rich would be guided to redistribute wealth with such gen-erosity that the outcome would be as though 'the earth had been divided into equal portions among its inhabitants'. Thus were laid the foundations of what has been called the 'culture of economism' – a culture in which economic factors are granted primacy 'as the main source of cultural meanings and values' (Collier and Esteban: 1998, 11).

It soon became obvious that the 'invisible hand' seemed inoperative in those regions of the globe which we have come to know as the 'third world'. The history of the relationship between Europe and these southern continents has 'from the outset been dominated by the self-interest of the West' (Goudzwaard: 1997, 108). As early as the sixteenth century we find Sir Francis Drake justifying the plunder of newly dis-covered lands in language that is profoundly disturbing: 'Their gain shall be in the knowledge of our faith, and ours *such riches as their country hath.*' Thus, from the Renaissance onwards, and with increasing determination after the industrial revolution, the peoples of Western

Europe sought to extend their political power in Asia, Africa and the Americas and a structure of economic imperialism developed which still dominates the relationship between the West and the nations of the third world.

The implications of this in relation to the Christian mission are obvious: the exploited areas of the world which have experienced the negative impact of Western economic expansion correlate exactly with the regions known to Christians as the traditional 'mission fields'. Yet, according to the economic historian Bob Goudzwaard, the Christian response to the entire development of modern society has been, in general, one of *synthesis* rather than prophetic protest. Not only did the hand of God become invisible in the nineteenth century but, in the area under discussion here, God's voice became almost inaudible. Consequently, 'both Christians and humanists are responsible for the presence of good and evil in the unfolding of the Western social order' (*ibid.*: 117).

The use of the term 'synthesis' to describe the relationship between Christianity and the culture of the modern West is significant. The churches prospered in this period (in more than one sense), and yet it is possible to argue that they did so through a process of accommodation to a culture that was increasingly secular. The American sociologist of religion Peter Berger has suggested that in the twentieth century churches in the United States were able to maintain a high level of allegiance in a society governed by secular values precisely because they provided religious legitimation for those values. For American Christians, says Berger, church membership

> in no way means adherence to a set of values at variance with those of the general society; rather it means a stronger and more explicitly religious affirmation of the same values held by the community at large. (Berger: 1961, 41)

Did something similar happen in Victorian Britain? R. H. Tawney believed that the emergence of what he called 'the acquisitive society' was possible precisely because the churches suppressed the social dimensions of the Gospel at those points where these would have led to a collision with the emergent materialist values. Christians accepted 'the popular assumption that the acquisition of riches was the main end of man' and the churches capitulated to what Tawney describes as 'the Gospel according to the Churches at Laodicea'. Christianity thus took an ideological form in which 'the power of religion in the individual soul is nicely proportioned to its powerlessness in society' (Tawney: 1961, 184).

The extent to which Christianity could be fused with the scientific and technological culture of the modern West can be illustrated in the language with which an enthusiastic advocate of Protestant missions anticipated the advance of civilisation across the world prior to the Great War. He rejoiced that 'steam and electricity have brought the world together' and claimed that the churches now controlled 'the power, the wealth, and the learning of the world' (MacDonald: 1910, 231). As to missions, they had left far behind them the unfortunate reputation for subversion which the authorities were inclined to believe as long as they were led by a Baptist cobbler. Now the missionary enterprise was being praised by eminent statesmen and the nations 'best fitted' to send missionaries around the globe are 'the strongest and most influential in the world', with empires dominating 'the greater part of the habitable globe' (*ibid.*: 219). This is, as Samuel Escobar has pointed out, simply a new version of the old imperial missiology, except that where the cross had accompanied the sword in the fifteenth century, it was now being used to bless and sanctify Western 'civilisation'.

There were, of course, courageous men and women who resisted this secularisation of the Gospel with great insight and vigour. Towards the end of his life Søren Kierkegaard launched a blistering attack on Christendom, exposing the hypocrisy of Protestant culture-religion and insisting that what went on in the Danish state church was a travesty of the Gospel of Christ. In England at exactly the same time, another 'prophet without honour', Edward Miall, had the temerity to suggest that at the very floodtide of their nineteenth-century influence, the British churches had lost contact with the teaching of the Gospel and had capitulated to a man-centred religion devoid of genuine spiritual power. In a remarkable book published in 1849, Miall accused wealthy British Christians of limiting their compassion to those far away, while ignoring the demands of justice and mercy in a society driven by the love of money:

> ... many a man who yearns for the conversion of the heathen at the antipodes, and subscribes liberally to send the gospel among them, evinces little or no compassion for the scarcely less degraded heathen at home. Foreign missions have passed through the stage of contempt and have even reached that of fashionable patronage.

> (Miall: 1849, 206–207)

25

Clearly, the historical and cultural contexts in which the two great waves of modern missions were launched in 1492 and 1792 contrast in the most striking manner with the social background of the apostolic mission recorded on the pages of the New Testament. The first evangelists could assume no political, economic or cultural advantages whatever and, for the best part of three hundred years, the churches were 'never secure against imperial enmity'. When Paul preached in Athens, or when he wrote to the young church at Rome, he did so with a degree of defensiveness, as though needing to justify his claims in the face of a massively powerful culture for which, at one level, he evidently feels respect. Kenneth Cragg has pointed out that Paul's mission always involved him in addressing his hearers from *within* a common culture, or even, from their perspective, from a position of *inferiority*, but never from a situation in which he was socially or culturally *above* them. 'From these beginnings it is a very far cry to the prestige context of Victorian Christian expansion ... where there were the assets of imperial connection' (Cragg: 1968, 41).

The End of Christendom and the Crisis of Modernity

I want to return to Hans Holbein's painting *The Ambassadors* with which this discussion of secularisation began. I suggested that in this great work Holbein expressed anxiety concerning the long-term impact of the new humanist learning both on individuals and at the level of Western culture. As we look back on the emergence of the modern world, how far have those premonitions been shown to be justified?

The historic turning point for modernity in Europe was, quite obviously, the First World War in 1914–18. On the night that war was declared, the British foreign secretary, Edward Grey, looking down Whitehall at dusk famously declared, 'The lamps are going out all over Europe'. Indeed they were and for many of those who survived the catastrophe it seemed as though the war had brought about the end of the known world. And yet, with the benefit of hindsight, we now know that what happened in 1914 was only 'the beginning of sorrows' and a seemingly endless catalogue of horrors have scarred the twentieth century. Eric Hobsbawm talks of 'living through a century of *religious* wars'. What he means by this becomes clear when he adds: 'Even those who advertised the pluralism of their own non-ideologies did not think the world was big enough for permanent co-existence *with rival secular religions*' (Hobsbawm: 1995, 5[emphasis mine]). Coming from a Marxist historian this is a remarkable statement and it may suggest to us that, just as the thirty years of religious war in Europe in the seventeenth century undermined the credibility of Christendom and led European thought and culture in a new direction, so the thirty years of mechanised warfare which devastated the continent in the twentieth century sounded the death knell for *modernity* and left us in greater need than ever of a new beginning. The seeds of postmodernity, with its characteristic suspicion of all the 'big stories', secular as well as religious, may actually have been sown in the trenches of France.

It is worth quoting at some length Hobsbawm's own considered conclusion at the close of his study of the twentieth century:

> We live in a world captured, uprooted and transformed by the titanic economic and techno-scientific process of the development of capitalism, which has dominated the past two or three centuries. We know, or at least it is reasonable to suppose, that we cannot go on *ad infinitum*. The future cannot be a continuation of the past, and there are signs, both externally, and, as it were, internally, that we have reached a point of historic crisis. The forces generated by the techno-scientific economy are now great enough to destroy the environment, that is to say, the material foundations of human life ... Our world risks both explosion and implosion. It must change. (*ibid.*: 584–5)

This would suggest that Hans Holbein's anxieties concerning the future of Western culture were more than justified. It will be recalled, however, that the artist's concern focused not only on society and culture, but on *people*; how would men and women cope in a world in which traditional sources of purpose and meaning were lost and the realities of life and death became too hard to bear? Could humankind actually survive the loss of faith and live in a world without transcendence? As we have seen, the Enlightenment philosophers had no doubt whatever concerning the answers to such questions. Indeed, in their view the removal of the chains of illusion forged by the superstitions of religion was a precondition for the emergence of a mature, responsible and universally happy human race. The enormous impact of the First World War can be judged when we set this untroubled confidence in human progress beside the language used by post-war writers who attempted to reflect on the meaning of the horrors they had witnessed in the trenches in France. Karl Krauss, writing in post-war Vienna, reflected the general mood in the title of his study, *The End of Humanity*, while the Russian philosopher Nicholas Berdyaev said that the war had been a 'revelation of the evil, hatred and jealousy' which had been previously concealed beneath the surface of a culture that had lost its capacity for moral judgements and had reduced people to little more than functionaries in a technical system. The loss of faith in God, said Berdyaev, had been followed by the loss of faith in man and 'the abyss yawned at the feet of mankind' (Berdyaev: 1935, 16). By the close of the twentieth century, Zygmunt Bauman could observe that while the project of modernity had proclaimed the release of human beings from all the 'constraints' imposed upon them by traditional societies, 'the liberated have been ushered into new, no less awesome slavery'. When the routes back to previous sources of meaning and purpose are sealed off, life comes to be defined as little more than 'the movement toward death . . . a long dress rehearsal of non-being' (Bauman: 1992, 49). We find ourselves here staring straight into the eyes of Holbein's troubled ambassadors.

Finally, what of Holbein's perception that the cross of Christ was becoming marginal in the new world then opening up through humanist scholarship and science? At the start of the third millennium a British social historian published a book with the title *The Death of Christian Britain*. The author rejected many of the conventional sociological accounts of the process of secularisation, arguing that Christianity had remained a significant cultural force in Britain well into the twentieth century. In Callum Brown's view the critical turning point was the decade of the 1960s when, quite suddenly, 'something very profound ruptured the character of the nation and its people, sending organized Christianity on a downward spiral to the margins of social significance' (Brown: 2001, 1). A religion that had shaped European culture for a thousand years, leaving its mark everywhere across the continent in architecture, symbols and institutions, suddenly found itself reduced to cultural irrelevance. Brown's conclusion, the more disturbing because of his rejection of ideologically based theories of secularisation, is stark:

> The cycle of inter-generational renewal of Christian affiliation, a cycle which had for so many centuries tied people however closely or loosely to the churches and to Christian moral benchmarks, was permanently disrupted in the 'swinging sixties'. Since then, a formerly religious people have entirely forsaken organised Christianity in a sudden plunge into a truly secular condition. (*ibid.*)

So then, does Holbein's remarkable painting anticipate the end of

Western Christianity, foretelling in the most extraordinary way the manner in which the Protestant religion would become, in the famous phrase, its own gravedigger? On the face of it, this seems to be the case. However, let us consider another painting by this artist, a picture painted in 1521 to which he gave the title *The Body of the Dead Christ in the Tomb* (picture 8). This is, in every sense of the word, a disturbing canvas. The viewer looks in at the side of the tomb where a life-size body, bearing the marks of torture and already displaying signs of decomposition, is stretched out. The depiction is entirely naturalistic, unrelieved by any sacred symbols and with no pointers which might suggest the transcendent meaning of this event. When the Russian novelist Dostoevsky viewed this painting in Basle he was completely overwhelmed by it. His wife feared that he was about to have an epileptic fit and she wrote that he could never forget the sensation he had experienced while gazing at a canvas which came to haunt him 'like a terrible nightmare' (Dostoevsky: 1955, 7). In fact, Dostoevsky refers to the painting many times in his novel *The Idiot*, where it becomes clear that he understood this work to pose a terrible threat to faith in Christ:

> . . . as one looks at the dead body of this tortured man one cannot help asking oneself the peculiar and interesting question: if such a corpse (and it must have been just like that) was seen by all his disciples . . . by the women who followed Him and stood at the cross . . . . how then could they possibly have believed, as they looked at the corpse, that the martyr would rise again? Here one cannot help being struck with the idea that if death is so horrible and the laws of nature are so powerful, then how can they be overcome? How can they be overcome when even He did not conquer them? (*ibid.*: 447)

Dostoevsky appeared to believe that Holbein's work was intended to be a kind of icon of secular humanism. More recent interpreters have reached the same conclusion, seeing in this picture 'no more than a dead body' (Carroll: 1993, 33). On this understanding the artist who placed the cross at the edge of the world-picture in *The Ambassadors*, had in fact earlier removed it altogether and announced, three centuries before Nietzsche, the death of God.

However, I suggest that this understanding of Holbein's work cannot be correct since the artist quite clearly intended to confess the faith of the Reformation in his art. In fact, as Derek Wilson says, 'No other picture expresses more eloquently the faith of the Reformation, the Christocentric faith of many humanists, the faith of those for whom the Bible had become a living book' (Wilson: 1997, 94). This is, to be sure, a Christ bereft of the sacred symbols which had become an integral part of the iconography of Christendom and, in that sense, it is deeply shocking to traditional piety. It is not surprising that Dostoevsky, steeped in Russian Orthodoxy, with its focus on the glory of the risen Christ, would find the realism of Holbein's art so alarming. Yet, as Wilson says, *The Body of the Dead Christ in the Tomb* amounts to a confession of faith 'from which non-essentials have been stripped in order to make truth more self-evident'. For Holbein the reality of the Word being made flesh meant that the body of Jesus really did suffer death: 'In the black secrecy of the tomb that flesh began to decay. Grasp this, Holbein says, and you begin to understand what the Incarnation is about' (*ibid.*: 95).

It is, I suggest, at precisely this point that we may catch a glimpse of the future for Christian theology and mission in a world in which the old civilisational landmarks are crumbling. One of the greatest tragedies of Christendom and of its missionary outreach around the globe concerns the manner in which it appropriated and subverted the symbol of the cross, turning that which spoke of the weakness and suffering of God into a sign which sanctified conquest and coercion in matters of faith. Peoples outside Christendom have frequently realised the enormity of the gap between the message of the suffering Messiah in the New Testament and the use made of the cross by a church which had learned how to be at home in a world shaped by ideologies inconsistent with the Gospel. For example, the great Jewish philosopher Martin Buber confessed near the end of his life that he had become a believer in Jesus Christ as the Messiah, but when asked why he did not declare himself to be a Christian, he replied that it was impossible for him to abandon his own people, and then added: 'I cannot see what the Christian Church as an institution has to do with Jesus Christ' (Kings: 2002, 270).

In Lahore, a statue of Queen Victoria which once stood at the major crossroads in the city can now be viewed in the local museum. Remarkably, the statue has been preserved intact, except that the cross on the orb in the imperial monarch's hand has been broken off. This may reflect the well-known Muslim rejection of the cross, but it is also a reminder 'that the cross cannot be properly used as a sign of empire, that human beings may not lord it over one another with the sign of the cross' (Lamb: 1982, 32).

At the end of Christendom, and with the dreams of the Enlightenment shattered by a century that has witnessed the growing dehumanisation of our species, the true meaning of Christ – understood so clearly by Hans Holbein – is capable of offering hope and renewal to a broken world. But for this to happen, that meaning must first be recovered within the life and practice of the church. A number of perceptive Jewish writers have pointed out that as for the first time in over sixteen centuries, Western Christians experience what it means to be powerless and despised, they may come to understand the bitterness of the marginalisation which Jews have always known within Christendom. Kenneth Cragg comments, 'If this brings the Church closer to the experiences which for centuries have tempered the soul of Jewry, *it may perhaps also release into new recognition the authentic dimensions of the Cross*' (Cragg: 1968, 116 [emphasis mine]).

I conclude this chapter with some moving lines written by Edward Shillito just after the First World War, which catch the mood of that time while also anticipating some of the major themes that were to occupy European theology later in the twentieth century:

> If we have never sought Thee, we seek Thee now;
> Thine eyes burn through the dark, our only stars;
> We must have sight of thorn-pricks on Thy brow,
> We must have Thee, O Jesus of the Scars.
>
> The heavens frighten us; they are too calm;
> In all the universe we have no place;
> Our wounds are hurting us; where is the balm?
> Lord Jesus, by Thy Scars, we claim Thy grace.
>
> The other gods were strong; but Thou wast weak;
> They rode, but Thou didst stumble to a throne;
> But to our wounds only God's wounds can speak,
> And not a god has wounds, but Thou alone.

3

A Biblical Model:
Israel between Exile and Return

In the previous chapter I attempted to describe the emerging new frontier for the Christian mission constituted by the *secularisation* of the Western world. Towards the end of that chapter I hinted that the demise of Christendom and the social marginalisation of the churches of Europe, which are invariably understood as negative developments when viewed from the religious perspective, can in fact be interpreted as offering a positive opportunity for Christian renewal and recovery. It is important to notice at this point that the notion of 'secularisation' is deeply ambivalent, not least because the roots of secular modernity may be discovered in the reaction against a world-dominating church which used coercion to enforce religious and ethical conformity. In the words of David Martin, 'the height of ecclesiastical power can be seen either as the triumph of the religious *or its most blasphemous secularis-ation*' (Martin: 1969, 55 [emphasis mine]). This explains why explicitly biblical accents can be detected in the voices of many of the secular prophets of the modern age, including Max Weber, Karl Marx and even Friedrich Nietzsche, since their demands for the liberation of humankind highlight Christendom's shameful neglect of its own charter documents.

However, while in the long term secularisation may be recognised as a providential opportunity for the recovery of the Gospel and the renewal of the church, at the present time it is more likely to be viewed as an almost unmitigated catastrophe. For many Western Christians it is spiritually and psychologically impossible to celebrate a situation in which, to quote a well-known English researcher, the churches are continually haemorrhaging members and the country seems to be full of people who 'used to go to church but no longer do' (Brierley: 2000,

236). In North America, long assumed to provide evidence capable of refuting the common assumptions about secularisation, all the indicators suggest that the churches are increasingly isolated from the emerging cultural consensus. 'We ring our bells,' says Darrell Guder, 'conduct our services . . . and wait for this very different world to come to us.' Pastors continue to preach sermons and carry on internal polemics over doctrine as though nothing outside has changed, but the reality is that *everything has changed* and the people 'are not coming back to the churches' (Guder: 2000, 95–6). Adjusting to this new context is incredibly difficult since the mindset of most Western Christians has been formed by centuries of tradition which has conditioned them to expect the surrounding world to constitute a friendly and hospitable environment for their beliefs and values. The consequences can be tragic:

> Like an ageing dowager, living in a decaying mansion on the edge of town, bankrupt and penniless, house decaying around her but acting as if her family still controlled the city, our theologians and church leaders [still] think and act as if we were in charge, as if the old arrangements were still valid. (Hauerwas and Willimon: 1989, 29)

In this difficult and painful context, help may be found by paying attention to a concept used within social anthropology to explain the process by means of which people in traditional societies make the transition from one stage of life to another. Victor Turner, following the work of Arnold van Gennep, discusses at some length the idea of *liminality,* the experience of being between statuses, neither one thing nor the other, a kind of *limbo* which is profoundly disorienting and troubling. People in a liminal stage, Turner says, feel 'as though they are being reduced or ground down to a uniform condition to be fashioned anew' (Turner: 1969, 95). For example, when boys belonging to a particular age-set reach the point at which they are to be initiated into manhood, they are separated from their mothers and isolated in a camp outside the village where they undergo training and preparation for the responsibilities that they must assume as mature men. During this time they are between statuses: no longer children, they have not yet become adults. They are in a *liminal* stage, which is, by definition, confusing and alarming.

Alan Roxburgh discusses the relevance of this concept to the understanding of the present situation facing Western Christianity and comments that, despite the feeling that we are in a dark tunnel, the present liminality 'offers the potential for a fresh missionary engagement in a radically changing social context' (Roxburgh: 1997, 27). Anthropological and historical studies demonstrate that liminal experiences, while involving human beings in much anguish and struggle, provide a context for growth and the discovery of newness and transformation. In relation to the present experience of Western Christians, which is one of finding themselves in an unexpected location at the margins of their own culture, Roxburgh observes,

> The only meaningful way forward lies in understanding and embracing our liminal experience. We must live with its confusion and humiliation, as a hopeful people ready to discover the new thing the Spirit will birth. The continued assumption of cultural symbols of power and success will only produce an inauthentic church with little gospel, much religion, no mission. (*ibid.*: 47)

In the remainder of this chapter I want to take up Roxburgh's observation that the biblical tradition is full of images and metaphors 'waiting for reappropriation in the unsettling land of liminality' (*ibid.*: 45). I wish to argue that the traumatic experiences of ancient Israel before, during and after the exile in Babylon involved precisely the kind of *liminality* described above and, as such, can provide us with a biblical-theological perspective which can help us as we strive to make sense of our times.

Israel Moving towards the Abyss

The confusion and despair felt by people in Israel as the known and established order collapsed is reflected in many of the psalms of lament. Perhaps the most tragic statement of all is the terrible cry of Psalm 74:9: 'We are given no miraculous signs, no prophets are left, and none of us knows how long this will be'. This is a quintessentially liminal experience – a long dark tunnel with no hint of light at its end. The same note is struck in the well-known exilic poem in which the exiles, asked to provide a song for their captors, retort: 'How can we sing the songs of the Lord in a foreign land?' (Psalm 139:4). The songs of Zion were not mere folk survivals that could be detached from the covenantal worldview within which they were embedded. Rather, for a people in exile they were painful reminders of what had been lost and it was impossible to sing them in a situation in which the whole of experienced reality seemed to make a mockery of the covenant faith. Such anguished cries of lament begin to resonate for Western Christians in the twenty-first century in a way they never did, and perhaps never could, during the long era of Christian dominance that has now come to an end.

In order to understand these biblical laments, including the extended outpouring of grief we know as the book of Lamentations, we must reflect on the terrible events that occurred in Jerusalem in the year 587 BC. In that year the Babylonians finally laid waste to the beloved city and brought to an end the Davidic dynasty. Everything that had been familiar was destroyed and for those who survived the tragedy it seemed as though the known world had come to an end. One such survivor invites God to pick his way through the 'everlasting ruins' and suggests that Yahweh might like to note that the invaders had systematically 'burned every place where God was worshipped in the land' (Psalm 74:3). We are dealing here not simply with one tragic event among others, but with an experience so seminal that it constitutes a pivotal point in the entire story of the Old Testament. In the period that witnessed the preaching of Israel's greatest prophets, the known world was dismantled and replaced with something quite new. Following Walter Brueggemann, I propose to take this as a *metaphor* through which we may be enabled to make sense of a similar process of transition in our own times, recognising that the biblical traditions spanning this period touch our situation very closely. We too face a point at which God appears to be terminating our known world and inviting us to a new world in which the true nature of the church and its mission can be recovered.

If the terrible events that occurred in the year 587 BC form a pivotal point in Old Testament history, the prophetic messages which both preceded and followed these events must be read in the light of them. That is to say, the *pre-exilic* prophets prepared the way for the ending of the known world, seeking to enable people to accept the loss of what had become familiar and beloved as being within the divine purpose, while those who preached *during and after* the exile summoned their hearers to receive with thankfulness the new world which God was bringing into being. As a result, on the one side of this great historical chasm the dominant note is a harsh one since the prophetic message deals primarily with judgement, destruction and loss. By contrast, on the other side of the cataclysm the prophetic tone is very different. With Zion a smoking ruin and a bewildered and lamenting remnant living as strangers in a land with a brilliant and powerful culture which owed nothing to their faith in Yahweh, the urgent and desperate need was for a new word of comfort and renewed vision and hope.

35

Clearly, there are dangers in attempting to draw parallels between the events described in the Old Testament and our situation today and I recognise the impossibility of a simplistic and uncritical appropriation of these texts. Nonetheless, we began this book with reflection on the unmistakable 'sense of an ending' that pervades the culture of the modern Western world at the dawn of the third millennium and this mood is very similar to that which is evident in the work of the great prophets of biblical Israel. Indeed, we have traced the historical connections between Christendom and Western civilisation that have resulted in the awareness of a *double* ending, the decay and decline of the churches in the West occurring in harness with the fading of the dreams and promises of the Enlightenment. Viewed from *outside* Christendom, the concurrence of the growth of missions and the spread of Western politico-economic power can look like a compromise so serious as to border on apostasy and it has led to demands from non-Western Christians for the unmasking of 'the secret alliance between the world missionary movement and the internationalist capitalist enterprise' (Costas: 1984, 69). Such a call, unwelcome and unpleasant though it may be for Western Christians, suggests that real parallels can be drawn between our current struggles to grasp the nature of the new patterns of Christian missionary obedience in a changing world, and the prophetic preaching of Isaiah, Jeremiah and Ezekiel in a period of radical transformation in ancient times. It may indeed be the case that 'the loss of the authority of the dynasty and the temple in Jerusalem is analogous to the loss of certainty, dominance, and legitimacy in our own time' (Brueggemann: 1986, 6). If so, it is not surprising that our present experience involves real mental and spiritual anguish, but the analogy also suggests that it is precisely in the acceptance and embrace of such painful dislocations that we may discover a new world gifted to us by the one who miraculously turns endings into surprising beginnings.

The Prophetic Critique of Religion

The most extended and substantial pre-exilic prophetic critique of the ruling ideology in Jerusalem is that found in the work of Isaiah. The great burden of his early prophecies concerns the corruption of religion and in chapter after chapter the prophet exposes and denounces the way in which religious belief and practice was used to *conceal* evil and injustice, while defending and *sanctifying* personal and social wickedness. At the level of both individual and social ethics, practices which involved obvious violation of the covenant faith of Israel were disguised by being granted an aura of holiness. Not surprisingly therefore, the tone of these chapters is harsh and relentless as the prophet repeatedly measures the life of his people against the standard of God's righteousness and finds it desperately wanting. This note is heard clearly in the opening chapter, which has been called the 'Great Assize'. Isaiah shows extraordinary courage in equating Jerusalem with Sodom and Gomorrah and repudiating the entire system of temple worship and liturgy as a worthless charade:

> When you come to meet with me,
> Who has asked this of you,
> This trampling of my courts?
> Stop bringing meaningless offerings!
> Your incense is detestable to me.
> New moons, sabbaths and convocations –
> I cannot bear your evil assemblies
>
> (Isa. 1:12–13)

The commentator Franz Delitzsch observed that God rejected this 'spiritless and undevotional tramping' to the temple *because it only wore out the floor* (Delitzsch: 1960, 91). In modern terms we might say that religion had become *secularised* – divorced from ethics, it was spiritually powerless and functioned as a screen concealing the violence and evil being practised daily within society. Scholars have used the phrase 'Royal-Temple Ideology' to describe the system of ritual and theology devised by an alliance of kings, priests and court-prophets to buttress their vested interests while violating the fundamental demands of Israel's covenant faith. Isaiah constantly reminded his hearers of the biblical vision of a society shaped by the demands of holiness and he predicted that when the kingdom of God finally arrived it would be characterised by 'justice and righteousness' (9:7). However, this eschatological hope stood in the sharpest possible contrast to the present reality which the prophet observed in Jerusalem where God 'looked for justice but saw bloodshed' and heard 'cries of distress' (5:7). The result was catastrophic: the land was dominated by what may be called a 'culture of economism' in which, in flagrant disregard of the Mosaic laws, property developers added house to house and joined 'field to field' (5:8). However, the growing prosperity of the privileged and powerful was, as always, accompanied by a deepening sense of the meaninglessness of life. The empty rituals in the temple did nothing to fill the spiritual vacuum at the heart of the culture, with the result that the city echoed night after night to the sounds of revellers at drunken parties as people 'stay up late at night until they are inflamed by wine' (5:11).

This prophetic analysis exposes the dark side of a culture with features that sound all too familiar to us: the mocking of everything sacred, the violation of every known taboo, and a moral relativism that involved transposing the ethical values of the covenant so that evil was classified as good and vice versa (5:20). Meantime, the endemic corruption of politics and the law left the poor marginalised and despairing of the institutions of the state (10:1–2). The situation was one in which faith was reduced to ideology, 'a symbolisation of life without any self-critical capacity, in which religion serves simply to legitimate the crassest vested interests that are operative' (Brueggemann: 1987, 33).

By the time Jeremiah appeared on the scene all hope of renewal and recovery had disappeared so that, to an even greater degree than his predecessor in Jerusalem, he found himself in unending conflict with the prevailing world-view. Like Isaiah, he saw beneath the surface of things and recognised the way in which religious language, including the familiar liturgies used in the temple, concealed and mystified moral and social reality. Those who held religious and political power used empty slogans which offered a false comfort to a suffering people:

> From the least to the greatest,
>> all are greedy for gain;
> prophets and priests alike,
>> all practise deceit.
> They dress the wound of my people
>> As though it were not serious.
> 'Peace, peace' they say,
>> when there is no peace.
> Are they ashamed of their loathsome conduct?
> No, they have no shame at all;
> They do not even know how to blush.
> So they will fall among the fallen;
>> They will be brought low when I punish them,
>>>> Says the Lord.
>>>> (Jer. 6:14–15)

On three occasions the prophet draws attention to his contemporaries' inability to blush, a condition that signals a cultural crisis in which 'all norms outside of self-interest have collapsed' (Brueggemann: 1987, 62).

And yet, despite this, the official position remained one of almost insane optimism; peace was declared to be the certain and continuing outcome as all the economic and social indicators were read in a positive manner. Against this, the lonely prophet, seeing through the deceit, was compelled to challenge such false confidence and to speak instead of the pain, loss and suffering which was being denied and suppressed by the official cover-up. This stance brought Jeremiah into inevitable collision with the establishment so that, in John Bright's moving words, the gates of Gethsemane opened before the prophet *contra mundum*, 'never to close again as long as he lived' (Bright: 1976, 165).

The most dramatic encounter between Jeremiah and those who represented the dominant ideology was that which occurred as the result of what has come to be called 'The Temple Sermon'. We have two accounts of this prophecy, one in chapter 7 and another in chapter 26. Delivered at the entrance to the temple, in the most prominent public forum in Jerusalem, it was a blistering attack on the entire system. Jeremiah quotes familiar and loved phrases from the temple liturgy and then dismisses these as 'deceptive words' (7:4). The deception lay in the belief that the mere existence of the temple in Jerusalem guaranteed the survival of the city and its protection from any and all military threats, irrespective of the moral condition of the nation. Against this, Jeremiah insists that the city and the temple will be utterly destroyed, becoming a heap of rubble like the sacred site at Shiloh before it. With extraordinary courage, he tears away the layers of camouflage which keep the system in place and announces that in reality the holy place has become *a robbers' cave* (7:11). This was an act of prophetic deconstruction in which the officially sanctioned optimism was exposed as lacking any true theological or moral foundation. Not surprisingly, the sermon almost cost Jeremiah his life since to the defenders of the status quo it was not merely theologically provocative but amounted to *an act of treason*. The idea that Zion might be destroyed was literally unthinkable since, within the prevailing world-view, certain promises made to the Davidic dynasty had been wrenched from their context and hardened into a nationalist dogma. The people had come to believe that '*this* nation, and *this* dynasty will always endure, for so God has promised' (Bright: 1976, 165). Jeremiah, by contrast, never forgot that the covenant had conditions as well as promises, that it contained curses as well as blessings, and that Yahweh remained sovereign, free and holy.

How do these prophetic texts relate to our similar, yet very different, historical situation? To use the language of hermeneutics, how might we fuse the two horizons found in the ancient Hebrew text, on the one hand, and our contemporary situation on the other? One way of building a bridge between the two contexts, ancient and modern, is through the recognition of the *ideological* function of religion in both situations. As we have seen, the mentality of those who held power in eighth-century Jerusalem was so wedded to the existing political system as to make the possibility that it might end literally unthinkable. This optimistic world-view was underwritten by an ideological form of religion which involved the radical perversion of Israel's covenant faith. As Christians in the modern Western world facing a time of endings, we must surely consider the question whether the loss of familiar patterns of church and mission is willed by God in response to our failure to maintain the purity of the Gospel. To be even more explicit: *has Christianity in the West been reduced to mere ideology, co-opted to serve the interests of movements largely at odds with the biblical vision of the world and its peoples?* The French scholar Jacques Ellul had no doubt as to the answer to these questions, arguing that 'Christendom astutely abolished Christianity by making us all Christians'. What came to be called 'Christianity' ceased to be 'an explosive ferment calling everything into question in the name of the truth that is in Jesus Christ' and became instead 'the structural ideology of this particular society' (Ellul: 1986, 39). The Christ who came to be the Lord and Saviour of every human culture was co-opted by one particular civilisation and was thus reduced to the role of guarantor of its values. Once captured and confined within the dominant and powerful culture of the West, Christ could be claimed as the inspiration for the crusades, the companion and sanctifier of the work of the *conquistadores*, or the baptiser of the project of secular modernity. Evangelicalism, originating in a movement of renewal which involved a summons to return to first principles, has not proved itself to be immune to the ideological virus that can infect and destroy all religious traditions. On the contrary, this movement has been 'deeply infiltrated by the spirit and tools of modernity' and it continues to act 'as one of the leading global apologists for modernity through its publications *and mission agencies*' (Seel: 1994, 308 [emphasis mine]). Granted this context, the pre-exilic prophets provide us with a crucial resource in the search for 'mission after Christendom' and they must be read with particular attention to the fact that faithfulness to the biblical vision will demand of us, as it did for Isaiah and Jeremiah, a willingness to face reality 'so that the God of endings can be confessed as Lord' (Brueggemann: 1978, 49).

At first glance the third great prophet in this period, Ezekiel, might appear out of place in this analysis. After all, he saw 'the visions of God' beside the Kebar River in Babylon and was thus a prophet in exile. However, Ezekiel's ministry straddled the great divide of 587 BC and a substantial section of his prophecies were delivered in the decade *before* the fall of Jerusalem. Indeed, this fact is crucial to the understanding of the book since the survival of the city, emptied of its most intelligent and gifted citizens (including, of course, Ezekiel himself), caused the insane optimism we have already noticed to resurface among the remnant that remained there. Ezekiel and his fellow exiles, removed to Babylon a decade before the fall of Zion, came to be viewed in Jerusalem as people who were under divine judgement, a kind of scum that had been removed in order that the true elect might survive and prosper in the holy city. In the blinkered view of this pathetic remnant, the rejection of the warnings of Isaiah and Jeremiah now appeared to be vindicated – Jerusalem had *not* fallen and hope sprung eternal that its glories would yet be restored. Jeremiah, still pursuing his lonely path within the city, was aware of this suicidal propaganda and wrote to the exiles in Babylon warning them against it. They should not listen to the false prophecies surfacing in Jerusalem, which suggested that their exile would soon be over and life in Judah would return to normal. On the contrary, they must settle down for a long stay:

> Build houses and settle down; plant gardens and eat what they produce. Marry and have sons and daughters; find wives for your sons and give your daughters in marriage so that they too have sons and daughters. Increase in number there, do not decrease. Also, seek the peace and prosperity of the city to which I have carried you in exile. Pray to the Lord for it, because if it prospers, you too will prosper. (Jer. 29:5–7)

Clearly, Jeremiah realised that God's future, which was yet to be revealed to his people, lay not in doomed Jerusalem, but *with the exiles.* Although despised by the self-righteous people who still clung to the past, it was these despised exiles, removed from the madness in Zion, who were hearing quite new things from God beside 'the rivers of Babylon'. Among these people, living in a strange land, real hope for the future was surfacing, a hope that was largely *discontinuous* with the old Jerusalem and all it represented. Jeremiah and his younger contemporary Ezekiel are at one on this, the letter from the old prophet in Jerusalem harmonising with and reinforcing the prophetic word delivered by the younger man in the swamplands of Babylon. Thus, Ezekiel is unequivocal in announcing that all hope of a return to the old Zion must be abandoned:

> The word of the Lord came to me: Son of man, this is what the sovereign Lord says to the land of Israel: *the end! The end* has come upon the four corners of the land. *The end* is now upon you . . .
>
> (Ezek. 7:1–3)

At the end of the 1960s the Christian apologist Francis Schaeffer wrote a book with the title *Death In The City*. Reflecting on his own experience Schaeffer said, 'It is a horrible thing for a man like myself to look back and see my country and my culture go down the drain in my own lifetime'. Drawing upon the prophetic texts we have examined here, Schaeffer concluded that one could only make theological sense of the present time in terms of an understanding of the reality of the *judgement* of God: 'Northern European culture is under the wrath of God' (Schaeffer: 1969, 13). Schaeffer showed remarkable courage and honesty in his unflinching embrace of reality, accepting the fact that a long era of Western history, an era that had witnessed many great things, was at an end. He recognised the relevance of Ezekiel's emphatic declaration 'The end!' to our times and also discovered, like the prophets, that the embrace of pain and loss opened a door to the discovery of a new hope and a fresh vision for the future. Thus, in *The Church at the End of the Twentieth Century* he suggested that the collapse of existing ecclesiastical and missiological models cleared the ground for a recovery of the apostolic understanding of the church and its mission in which the authentic mark of Christians – mutual love – would again become central to Christian identity. Schaeffer would have agreed with Walter Brueggemann that the churches of the West can move through a time of great change 'with relief and gratitude that we are not summoned to be an echo of culture, either to administer its economics, to embrace its psychology, or to certify its morality. To us is gifted an alternative way.' (Brueggemann: 1987, 105–7).

Israel on the Cusp of Radical Newness

If pre-exilic prophecy involves the critique of ideology and the revelation of God's freedom and judgement, that which follows the exile strikes a very different note. This is evident in the familiar language of the so-called 'Book of Comfort':

Comfort, comfort my people
    says your God.
Speak tenderly to Jerusalem
    And proclaim to her
That her hard service has been completed,
    That her sin has been paid for,
    That she has received from the Lord's hand
    Double for all her sins.

                (Isa. 40:1)

The prophetic word is here addressed, not to people who are manipulating religion in their own interests, but rather to those who are crushed and broken, to the despairing exiles who are bereft of hope. These people need no preacher to remind them that the end has come; the exiles, the *diaspora*, are in danger of drifting, rudderless and without a compass, in very strange and dangerous waters.

Two great dangers threatened the covenant faith of Israel at this time. On the one hand there was the threat of *insular traditionalism*. The complaints we hear being expressed in this chapter, that the way of the exiles is hidden from Yahweh and their cause is disregarded by him (40:27), appear to reflect this negative response to the experience of exile. The laments uttered in the immediate aftermath of the destruction of Jerusalem, some of which we noticed earlier in this chapter, and the terrible agonies of those who were carted off in chains to Babylon, have here hardened into a liturgical *tradition* which marginalises praise and thanksgiving. Put very crudely, this is the option of the ghetto, the attempt to survive in an alien context through a developing tradition of worship that involves a morbid remembrance of the tragedies which befell an earlier generation. The irony is that, whereas the pre-exilic prophets had to combat an optimism which privileged celebration in worship and suppressed grief, the problem here is to counter a ritualised mourning which excludes the possibility of fresh hope and blinds God's people to the wonderful new things just about to come over the horizon.

The conclusion we need to draw at this point is that both the tradition of *lament* in the face of terrible loss and suffering, and that of *celebration* in the discovery of God's ultimate purpose have their place in the experience of the believing community. Pain and loss must not be denied but brought to expression in the presence of the living God. But equally, lament cannot be the final word, but is the means through which we are enabled to discover divine new beginnings. The prophetic message, taken as a whole, underlines the necessity of both these traditions: lament alone extinguishes hope and blinds us to God's newness; celebration without tears is false and incapable of bringing release to those who suffer. Only those who know real anguish will sing new songs, and without anguish 'the new song is likely to be strident and just more royal fakery' (Brueggemann: 1978, 79).

The second great danger was quite different; we may call it *cultural assimilation*. As the years passed and new generations grew up in Babylon who had never seen Jerusalem or known by personal experience the agonies of the past, the possibility grew that what had once seemed like a strange and alien culture would come to be viewed as 'home'. Indeed, as we have seen, Jeremiah had encouraged the exiles to settle in this country and his words might easily be read as suggesting that Babylon was indeed the locus for the fulfilment of the divine purposes. If, as the prophets had repeatedly insisted, the Babylonians were the agents of Yahweh's purposes, there was a certain logic in concluding that Babylonian culture was vindicated and its religion and politics shown to be of superior value. For their part the Babylonians were not slow in interpreting their military triumphs as marking 'the end of history' and in trumpeting the definitive and absolute nature of their imperial system. In such a context, the exiles might easily begin to acquiesce in the policy of the 'cultural melting pot', retaining symbolic reminders of their ethnic origins but accepting that their identity as people was now, in all important respects, Babylonian.

The post-exilic prophets are concerned to address both these dangers. In particular, Babylonian religion and politics are subjected to a prophetic critique as searching and profound as that with which Isaiah and Jeremiah exposed weaknesses in Jerusalem. It needs to be stressed here that the rationale for this critique is not to be found in a constitutional tendency of prophets to adopt counter-cultural stances, but rather must be understood in relation to the opportunity that a chastened and purified Israel has to actually hear of the new thing that God is about to accomplish. What is coming into view is something radically different from both Jerusalem and Babylon; the revelation of a kingdom which transcends the passing achievements of any and all merely temporal, political arrangements. Thus, the familiar words of Isaiah 55:1–3 need to be heard in the context of Babylon's staggering political and economic success:

Come, all you who are thirsty, come to the waters;
and you who have no money, come, buy and eat!
Come, buy wine and milk, without money and without cost.
Why spend money on what is not bread,
And your labour on what does not satisfy?
Listen, listen to me, and eat what is good,
And your soul will delight in the richest of fare.

(Isa. 55:1–3)

Here is a clash between the word of God and a culture which, while visibly successful, is built on an idolatry that reduces human beings to mere consumers of material benefits provided by the imperial system. The exiles are warned that they cannot live by Babylonian bread alone, however good and plentiful it may be. Indeed, the prophet subjects Babylonian religion to a devastating exposure (chapter 46) and, in language that is highly subversive of the imperial power, indicates that this seemingly impregnable system will suffer complete collapse (chapter 47). The exiles are to remember that they are precisely that – aliens in a strange land – and, raising their expectations beyond the horizon provided by a failing empire, they must prepare themselves for nothing less than a reign of righteousness that will embrace the whole earth and culminate in cosmic renewal (65:17–25).

I want to suggest that, just as the metaphor of 'exile' can be appropriated by modern Christians in the ways already indicated, so too the metaphor of 'return' found in the post-exilic prophets has a particular resonance and application to our times. In these remarkable texts (and we should include here passages like Jeremiah 33 and Ezekiel 33–48) Israel is restored to faith by a retelling of the old story that enables them 'to confront their despair rather than be surrounded by it'. In the context of a brilliant pagan culture which appears successful in its own terms, they are gifted an alternative consciousness, one which makes genuine humanness possible. This prophetic vision of God's new future utterly transcends the possibilities available in Babylon, but it also moves beyond the confines of Israel's pre-exilic faith with a glorious vision of redemption that extends to the ends of the earth and the furthest reaches of space and time.

On 23 July 1933, Dietrich Bonhoeffer preached a sermon based on the text Matthew 16:13–18, in which Jesus declares to the apostle Peter, 'on this rock I will build my church, and the gates of Hades will not overcome it'. Bonhoeffer's situation in a Nazi-dominated Germany was becoming critical. Indeed, on the very day that this sermon was preached, the 'German Christians' who advocated the path of accommodation with the Nazis won a crushing victory which resulted in the official churches actively pursuing a synthesis between the Gospel and the ideology of National Socialism. Bonhoeffer and those who stood with him in the Confessing Church, were unalterably opposed to such compromise, insisting that the confession of the Lordship of Christ demanded resistance to the idolatrous claims of the Nazis. This is the context in which Bonhoeffer spoke the following words, which, I suggest, have an extraordinary relevance to our situation today and relate very closely to the challenges we face in a secularised culture dominated by false ideologies and powerful idols:

> But it is not we who build. He [Christ] wills to build the church. No man builds the church but Christ alone. Whoever is minded to build the church is surely well on the way to destroying it; for he will build a temple to idols without wishing or knowing it. We must confess – he builds. We must proclaim – he builds. We must pray to him – he builds. We do not know his plan. We cannot see whether he is building or pulling down. It may be that the times which by human standards are times of collapse are for him the great times of building. It may be that the times which from a human point of view are great times for the church are times when it is pulled down. It is a great comfort which Christ gives to his church: you confess, preach, bear witness to me, and I alone will build where it pleases me. Do not meddle in what is my province. (Bonhoeffer: 1970, 212)

4

Finding the New Frontiers:
(2) The Challenge of Pluralisation

In the previous chapters we have traced the changes that occurred *within* European culture as the medieval world-view was replaced by those new ways of understanding the cosmos and humankind to which we have attached the label 'modernity'. The momentous nature of these changes and their potential for both good and evil was recognised, I have suggested, by artists like Hans Holbein. However, if radical change was occurring within Europe, the so-called 'age of discovery' *beyond* this continent brought a deluge of new information and a series of encounters with previously unknown peoples which so overloaded the medieval world-picture as to accelerate its collapse. Only two years before Holbein painted *The Ambassadors*, Francisco Pizarro had conquered the Inca empire in what we now know as Peru, murdering the king, Atahualpa, after forcibly converting him to Catholicism. Later, one of the *conquistadores* was to reflect on the wonders of the ancient civilisation he had helped to destroy: 'Where have men ever seen the things they have seen here?' Why, he wondered, had God allowed something so great to remain hidden from the rest of the world for so long?

Such admiration for Inca or Aztec civilisations was rare among the conquerors, who were inclined to view the native peoples of South America as a sub-human species whose only hope lay in their enforced incorporation within Christendom. The Spanish theologian, Juan de Sepulveda, fatefully extended the medieval justification for the pursuit of a just war to cover the violence and brutality of the conquest, arguing that 'it is just and natural that prudent, honest and humane men should rule over those who are not so' (Richard: 1990, 62). For Sepulveda the ends – conversion to a church which provided exclusive access to grace and salvation – justified violent means; it was, he said, 'thanks to terror combined with preaching' that the Indians had become Christians. A contemporary Chilean theologian says that such ideological reasoning left the biblical faith stranded 'on the fringe of the exercise of domination' and eventually destroyed the credibility of European Christendom in South America (Richard: 1990, 63). At the same time, prophetic voices were raised in the New World by missionaries who insisted that the Gospel provided a perspective from which colonial domination could be critiqued and resisted. Indeed, missionaries like Bartholomé de Las Casas and Fray Antonio de Montesinos vigorously opposed oppression and articulated a theological perspective which recognised the positive value of other cultures. The traditional world-views of indigenous peoples could, rightly understood, enlarge European knowledge of the activity of God within the human family and a genuine, freely chosen meeting of such peoples with the living Christ might reveal previously hidden dimensions of the grace of the Gospel. In other words, cross-cultural mission done in a manner that reflected the humble and crucified Messiah, became *the learning experience of the Western church.*

The Ideology of Christendom

As we have already seen, the roots of the medieval model of mission, which was transferred to South America with such catastrophic results in the fifteenth century, can be traced back to the emergence of Christendom. The influence of this imperial missiology can often be recognised in the architecture, symbolism and art of ancient European church buildings. Consider, for example, the French town of Albi in the region of Languedoc in the south-west of the country. It is dominated by a cathedral church, which, in its unique and disturbing appearance, is like no other. Viewed from the outside it looks like a cross between a fortress and a warehouse, its unadorned walls rising like a vertical cliff-face to an enormous height and conveying the impression of a cold, utilitarian building, designed to protect those *inside*, rather than to attract anyone from the outside. However, for modern tourists determined to explore the interior of this strangest of medieval cathedrals, the biggest shock is yet to come. No sooner has one entered the building than the eyes are drawn, as if by a magnet, toward the murals which dominate the front of this huge basilica. The attractive power of these paintings lies not in their beauty (for they have none), but rather in their oddness and their ability to shock modern sensibilities. What the viewer sees, in endless and minute detail, is a depiction of the physical agonies endured by the damned in the flames of hell. Consequently, the interior of this church offers no relief or contrast from its daunting and depressing exterior but rather, by a grotesque representation of an eternal chamber of horrors, it increases one's sense of unease and alarm. If the architectural design of the building was intended to repel outsiders (and it was), then the murals which filled the gaze of worshippers inside were a means to enforce conformity to the Catholic faith by instilling terror in the souls of any who might be contemplating defection. Here is the doctrine of hell, understood in the most literal manner, used as an instrument of social control.

The clue to the historical circumstances that produced this most unlovely of churches is to be found in the name of this town, a name made famous in the designation of the heretical group that once attracted up to 40,000 adherents in this region, the *Albigenses*. This type of religion, promoting a dualist form of belief in opposition to Roman Catholic orthodoxy, was found in scattered locations across southern Europe throughout the Middle Ages. Such underground religious movements challenged the mainstream church both at the level of theological belief and, perhaps more seriously, in the area of ethical principles and practice. Albigensians (also called Cathars) and the more orthodox Waldensians, offered alternative definitions of the Christian faith to that which came from Rome and they understood the demands of discipleship in ways that were radically different. Cathars, for example, were pacifists and vegetarians, they refused to take public oaths and taught that the death penalty was invalid. This was a religion of the poor: renouncing feudal hierarchy, it insisted on a modest lifestyle for its members and imposed no tithes on those who joined it. Not surprisingly, therefore, it attracted much support in the south of France, where it resisted and challenged the hegemony of the Roman Catholic Church. Cathar preaching constantly focused attention on the contrast between the model of discipleship presented by its leaders and that found within the Catholic mainstream: 'There are two churches: one flees and forgives (Matt. 10:22–3); the other possesses and burns' (Brenon: 1997, 69).

In 1209, in response to the express wish of Pope Innocent III, a crusade against the Albigeois was declared and for nine years Catholic armies ravaged the country in an attempt to eliminate this rival faith. Hans Küng comments that this war against dissenting believers led to the extermination of large segments of the population, 'put the cross to shame, and was a perversion of Christianity' (Küng: 1995, 399). This is the background to the building of the cathedral at Albi; the church could survive in a region seething with dissent only by becoming a literal fortress able to withstand the enemies outside the walls, while terrifying its members within.

The use of armed force to ensure the unchallenged dominance of the Catholic faith was consistent with the 'medieval paradigm of mission'. Within this paradigm 'truth' was understood in terms of orthodox belief as this was defined within the Catholic Church and 'salvation' became inseparable from membership within that institution. Medieval Catholicism thus laid claim to the exclusive possession of both truth and grace and the mission of the church became equated with the extension of ecclesiastical power. Such a view allowed no place for pluralism in theology, let alone in religion. The roots of this imperial missiology can be traced back to Augustine who, in the controversy with the Donatists in North Africa, justified coercion in evangelisation, developing an argument which was to have fatal, if unintended, consequences, that such compulsion was consistent with the teaching of Jesus. The words of Christ recorded in Luke 14:23 – 'compel them to come in' – were read in a literal fashion so that, by a perverse interpretation, the use of armed force came to be understood as an expression of the compassion of Jesus!

By the Middle Ages, with Christendom hemmed into its European heartlands by a militant Islam and so sealed off from contact with the rest of the world, the seeds planted by church fathers like Augustine and Cyprian hardened into an exclusivistic dogma. In 1441 the Council of Florence declared: 'Not only pagans but also Jews, heretics, and schismatics will have no share in eternal life'. The murals in Albi cathedral might have been painted to illustrate the dogma promulgated at this council: 'They will go into the eternal fire . . . unless they become aggregated to the Catholic Church before the end of their lives'. David Bosch observes that although the explicit appeal to Luke 14:23 eventually fell into disuse, the sentiment behind it persisted well into modern times and, we may add, was subtly to influence Protestant views of mission and of the fate of peoples who came to be classified as *unreached*.

1. Stanley Spencer, *Christ Carrying the Cross* (1920). (Tate Britain, London.)

2. Hans Holbein the Younger (1497/8–1543), *The Ambassadors* (1533), (oil on panel). (National Gallery, London.)

3. William Blake, *Newton* (*c.* 1795). (Tate Britain, London.)

4. William Blake, *Nebuchadnezzar* (*c.* 1795). (Tate Britain, London.)

5. [left] Hieronymus Bosch (*c*.1450–1516), *The Garden of Earthly Delights*, first
   panel (*c*.1500) (oil on panel). (Prado, Madrid.)
6. [centre] Hieronymus Bosch (*c*.1450–1516), *The Garden of Earthly Delights*,

second panel (*c.*1500)(oil on panel). (Prado, Madrid.)

7. [right] Hieronymus Bosch (*c.*1450–1516), *The Garden of Earthly Delights*, third panel (*c.*1500)(oil on panel). (Prado, Madrid.)

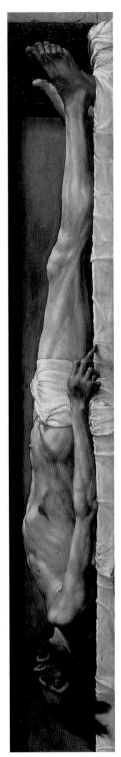

8. Hans Holbein the Younger, *The Body of the Dead Christ in the Tomb* (1521). (Oeffentliche Kunstsammlung Basel.)

9. Hieronymus Bosch (*c.*1450–1516), *Christ Mocked (The Crowning with Thorns)* (*c.*1490–1500)(oil on panel). (National Gallery, London.)

10. Georges Rouault, *Christ in the Outskirts* (1920–24). (Bridgestone Museum of Art, Ishibashi Foundation, Tokyo.)

Mission as the Learning Experience of the Church

We have already noticed how missionaries like Fray Antonio de Monte-sinos and Bartholomé de Las Casas who went to South America in the fifteenth and sixteenth centuries rediscovered a biblical model of mission which provided them with a critical perspective on their own culture and led them to defend the victims of oppression and colonis-ation. Actually, it is possible to discover such alternative, contextual approaches to mission much earlier in the history of the church. In the middle of the thirteenth century a Dominican monk who was endeav-ouring to pioneer a dialogical, non-violent approach to Muslims in Spain wrote to Thomas Aquinas pleading for help. The monk had explicitly rejected the violence of the crusades, yet he was puzzled that his own approach, relying on preaching, had met with little success. How could Christians share the Gospel with people whose religion seemed to predispose them to reject it? Aquinas responded with his famous *Summa contra Gentiles* in which he sought to pioneer an approach to Islam that not only abandoned the use of physical violence, but also repudiated forms of preaching that reduced mission to a shouting match in which genuine communication became impossible. Like his correspondent, Aquinas abhorred physical coercion, but he went further in recognising that mission employing verbal proclamation might still adopt a *crusading style*. By contrast, the *Summa* sought for points of contact with Islam, endeavouring to meet the other faith where it was strong and acknowledging the truth of the central Muslim affirmation of the unity and oneness of God. Once having established this common ground, the Christian story might be imaginatively retold in such a way that it related to the perceived gaps and unfulfilled longings within Muslim experience.

Let us go back even earlier, to AD 716. In that year the English missionary known to history as Boniface crossed the North Sea to begin work in Frisia. Three years later he directed his attention toward Saxon, pagan peoples and, repudiating the gentler methods of earlier Celtic missionaries in this area, conducted a campaign designed to replace traditional, primal beliefs with the Roman faith. The most famous inci-dent in Boniface's career concerns the destruction of the sacred oak tree at Geismar. His biographer describes the incident as follows:

> As he, strengthened by unswerving determination, cut the tree down, there was a great number of pagans present who kept on cursing

this enemy of their gods under their breath with the greatest fervor. (Quoted in Murphy: 1989, 14)

This incident has often been described as a key turning point in the evangelisation of the Saxon people and among Protestants it is sometimes presented as a model of the so-called 'power encounter' through which the spiritual forces of paganism are said to be routed and the lordship of Christ is established. However, the reference to the large crowd of Saxons barely concealing their anger at this act of desecration, and the fact that Boniface was able to fell the oak only with the protection of Frankish soldiers who stood ready to crush any local resistance, suggests that the victory won here was superficial rather than real. At the time, says Ronald Murphy, the triumph of Christianity seemed so self-evident to the conquerors that there seemed 'little need to worry about German hearts and minds' (Murphy: 1989, 14).

The fact is that the Saxons, like the Cathars and Waldensians, were the objects of an imperial missionary practice in which the crucifix and the sword operated together as instruments of conquest and oppression. Indeed, Murphy suggests that the thirty-three-year war of conversion and conquest which Charlemagne waged against the Saxon people in northern Germany was the most brutal page in the entire history of the Christianisation of Europe. However, there were Christians who realised that such methods were inconsistent with the Gospel of Jesus Christ and were doomed to failure as long as the needs of *Saxon hearts and minds were ignored*. In other words, they understood that merely superficial changes in behaviour, enforced at the point of the sword, created an external conformity which concealed a profound loathing for the conquerors and actually stiffened internal adherence to traditional beliefs and values.

One such Christian was the unknown author of an extraordinary ninth-century work entitled *Heliand* – a Saxon term meaning 'saviour'. This masterpiece of ancient epic poetry retold the Gospel story within the context of the traditional Saxon world-view. The author clearly felt profound sympathy for the oppressed Saxons and he presents a Jesus who enters deeply into the Saxon world in order to become its true Saviour. The *Heliand* is thus a profoundly counter-cultural document, its Christ stands over against the alien Jesus of the conquerors who came only to destroy the traditional world and replace it with another. Ronald Murphy observes that the unknown author of the *Heliand* achieved what might have been thought impossible:

He remained faithful to the orthodox Christian teaching of the Gospel, and yet in his contemplation of that Gospel imagined an almost unthinkably new and different form of Christianity, thereby transforming the Gospel into the traditional religious imagery and values of his people.

(Murphy: 1989, ix)

The writer of the *Heliand* rejected the confrontational missiology of Boniface together with the ideological use of Christianity in support of Frankish imperialism. That is to say, he recognised the *translatability* of the message of the Gospel and affirmed the validity of local expressions of Christian faith and discipleship. The Christ of the *Heliand* enters the Saxon world as both the judge and redeemer of its culture, challenging ideas and values inconsistent with the kingdom of love and justice he has revealed, while yet affirming and transforming those elements of the primal world-view which were crucial to Saxon Christian identity. In its skilful use of ideas and imagery drawn from the primal world of this north-European people, the *Heliand* is, in Murphy's phrase, a 'North Sea Gospel'.

The following passage provides an example of the way in which, through the use of Saxon language and symbolism, the *Heliand* managed to relate the events of the Gospel (in this case, the birth of Jesus) to the suffering and oppression being experienced by its readers:

At that time the Lord God had granted to the Roman people the greatest kingdom, had strengthened the hearts of their army so that they had subdued many a nation. They had, from Fort Rome, won an empire, those comrades under helmet; their military governors ruled in every land, had power over the people, in every foreign nation.

(Quoted in Murphy: 1989, 20)

Not for the last time, an oppressed and suffering people read the Gospel and felt the cultural and historical gulf which divided them from first-century Palestine evaporate: they are *there* when the Saviour is born among a people dominated by a militaristic power which threatens their deepest beliefs and values. Yet more wonderful, he is *here* – no longer an alien Christ endorsing the world-view of the oppressor and so the enemy of everything that is loved and valued, but a humble, gentle Messiah who is tempted in the 'deep forest' and knows and subdues the terrors of the ever-threatening seas.

The *Heliand* thus provides us with an early example of cross-cultural mission as *the learning experience of the church*. In the process of communicating the good news of Christ across a cultural barrier, the missionary discovers a legitimate theological pluralism that, far from threatening the integrity of the Gospel, actually enhances it. The courage and boldness of Boniface is not in doubt, but his confrontational approach to mission, which has been imitated repeatedly across the centuries, is fatally flawed because *it makes the culture of the missionary inseparable from the message he brings*. When this happens then the Gospel is liable to be perceived by those to whom it is offered not as 'good news' at all, but rather as the announcement that Christ is implacably *against* the receptor culture. Mission of this kind is incapable of relating adequately to human cultural and religious realities, yet its failure often triggers a search for different approaches and so leads to the recovery of the apostolic model found on the pages of the New Testament. The approach of the author of the *Heliand* is, after all, patterned on the example of the earliest disciples of Jesus who, as the book of Acts so clearly shows, moved *from* a position in which religion was intertwined with a particular ethnic and cultural identity, *to* one in which the central task became that of *translating* the Gospel into ever new languages and cultures. As we shall see in the next chapter, this radically new understanding of mission came about only after an immense and protracted struggle, yet once established it involved an apostolic commitment to 'the *pluralist merit of culture within God's universal purpose* (Sanneh: 1990, 1 [emphasis mine]).

In 1806 a young Englishman aged 25 arrived in India. His name was Henry Martyn and the story of his tragically brief service on the subcontinent provides us with a classic example of cross-cultural mission as the learning experience of the church from the first generation of modern, Protestant missions. Like the author of the *Heliand* and the Catholic missionaries who opposed the racism and violence of the *conquistadores*, Martyn found himself in a context of political and religious conflict in which the culture of those he wished to reach was under threat from a powerful and invasive nation with which he himself was identified. Martyn's journals record in detail his agonised wrestling with the ambiguities of his situation as a paid agent of the power responsible for the plunder of India. 'A man who has unjustly got possession of an estate hires me as a minister to preach to his servants and pays me a salary' he writes, 'the money wherewith he pays me comes unjustly to him, but justly to me' (Cragg: 1992, 18).

To this great source of inner conflict was soon added another which came to dominate his thoughts throughout the remainder of his brief life. Martyn was a brilliant linguist who arrived in Asia with the conviction that if he could master Urdu, Hindi, Sanskrit, Bengali and Arabic and ensure the translation of the Bible into these tongues then Hindus, Buddhists and Muslims would have ready access to the truth of the Gospel. It did not take long, however, before he realised that the task of 'translation' required much more than linguistic abilities. Cultural, religious and theological factors stood in the way of communication to a degree that Martyn had never anticipated before leaving the shores of Britain. Mission in India involved covering territory never traversed by the writer of the *Heliand* for this was mission far *beyond* Christendom, where the corresponding terms and idioms, which made a contextualised Saxon version of the Gospel possible, simply seemed to be unavailable. To his diary Martyn confessed that he could not work out how the apostle Paul would have acted in his position. The New Testament demonstrated beyond question the validity of the task of translation and it supplied concrete examples of apostolic boldness in making Christ known to Greeks, but *where did India fit into this picture?* Where could one find an entrance for Christ into this religiously plural world in which centuries of tradition had created cultures in which even the most basic Christian concepts were liable to be misunderstood?

For example, the notion of the 'new birth', so central to the Evangelical movement in Britain that had supplied the motivation for the missionary movement as well as its personnel, was heard by Hindus within a religious framework which led to it being understood in terms of *reincarnation*. Of course people *had* to be born again, the accumulated load of *karma* made rebirth inevitable and locked human beings into an endless cycle of death and rebirth. Elsewhere in Asia, a Buddhist could read the Gospels consecutively and marvel that Jesus managed to achieve *nirvana* after only four rebirths! Little wonder then that while Henry Martyn never doubted that he was in possession of the 'pearl of great price' he found himself 'in an Indian/Persian market where that supreme treasure was, somehow, no pearl at all' (Cragg: 1992, 29). Consequently, Martyn was compelled to re-evaluate his perception of mission:

> What suprises me is the change of views I have here from what I had in England. There my heart expanded with hope and joy at the prospect of the speedy conversion of the heathen. But here the sight of the apparent impossibility requires a strong faith to support the spirits.
>
> (Quoted in Cragg: 1992, 23)

Martyn's reference to his surprising change of views echoes language used by his friend and colleague in India, William Carey. The man often called the 'father' of modern missions had also arrived on the sub-continent convinced that Hinduism would quickly give way before the preaching of the evangel. Yet after years of relatively fruitless labour Carey recognised that 'we may be only as pioneers to prepare the way for more successful missionaries' (Carey: 1801, 75). Another member of the 'Serampore triumvirate', William Ward, wrote to an American correspondent twenty years later and confessed that the 'restricted progress of Christianity . . . notwithstanding the Son of Righteousness has arisen . . . forms one of the most mysterious dispensations of Providence that has ever occupied human attention' (Ward: 1821, 34). These are voices from the first generation of modern Protestant missionaries confessing that they have learned from painful experience that evangelisation outside Christendom involved problems of communication unheard of at home, and that in this religiously plural world the identification of the Gospel with Western culture only served to increase the confusion and misunderstanding.

In 1810, already weakened by illness, Henry Martyn determined to make his way back to Britain overland in order to supervise the publication of his Urdu New Testament. He travelled via the famed Persian city of Shiraz, then made his way to Isfahan, Teheran and Tabriz. This final journey involved a massive encounter with Islam which raised the same kind of perplexing questions that we have already seen him articulating in relation to Indian religious traditions. He died on 16 October 1812 in Tokat, leaving as his legacy the journal in which, perhaps more than any other modern missionary, he confessed 'the painful perplexity of registering the sheer otherness of faiths' (Cragg: 1992, 30).

The unknown author of the *Heliand*, Catholic missionaries like Ramon Lull in North Africa, Bartholomé de Las Casas in South America, and Matteo Ricci in China, together with the Protestant pioneers in India to whom reference has just been made, all would bear witness to the fact that the encounter between the Gospel and cultures is (to paraphrase Paul) a schoolmaster to lead us to a deeper knowledge of the grace of God in Jesus Christ. What is more, that process of discovery is ongoing, so that wherever the Gospel is transmitted across a cultural barrier the potential exists for the revelation of some quite new dimension of divine grace as Jesus comes to be known and loved in 'every nation, tribe, people and language'. True cross-cultural mission thus widens our perspectives and involves the renunciation of all forms of ethnocentrism. It creates the possibility of what René Padilla has called 'theological cross-fertilization among different cultures' since, through the work of the Holy Spirit, 'each culture has something to contribute in connection with the understanding of the gospel and its implications for the life and mission of the church' (Padilla: 1985, 36).

Take the case of the Qom people who live in the Gran Chaco of Argentina. The Qom are a traditional, tribal people who could be taken as representative of the millions of primal peoples throughout the world whose ancient ways of life are in danger of disappearing under the impact of modernity. The Qom world-view contrasts with that of the modern West at many points. They do not regard 'truth' as something that is discovered by a process of logical deduction, it is rather to be found in the tension between seemingly contradictory perspectives. The Qom share with the vast majority of the human race throughout history the notion that human identity is related to the integration of the individual within the group, so that the nature and purpose of humankind is defined socially, never individualistically. In such a society the fundamental value is that of maintaining balance, of ensuring harmony and oneness within the family, the clan, and within those widening circles of relationships that extend ultimately across the dividing line of death and into the unseen (but real) world. The Qom know how different their world is from that which is shaped by modernity and, despite conversion to Christianity, they are not about to abandon traditional values. As one of their elders puts it: 'We must . . . be strong in our own culture, because the civilized world has failed. We know where the civilized world is headed, *and it is useless*' (Horst: 2001, 179 [emphasis mine]).

Another Qom Christian pastor, reflecting on the pattern of life he had observed among his grandparents, noted that for them the sharing of scarce resources among all who had need was simply taken for granted. Their *conduct* thus revealed that they were not strangers to the love of God, whereas he concludes that missionaries who demand, on the basis of their reading of certain Pauline texts, that Qom Christians must abandon traditional ways and accept employment in a wage-based economy, seem not to be behaving in a manner that is consistent with that divine love (*ibid.*: 169).

For the Qom, as for the Saxons in ninth-century Europe, a mass movement toward Christianity resulted not in the abandonment of traditional culture, but in its *revitalisation*. A dispirited people,

threatened with the destruction of their known world by the encroach-
ment of a highly sophisticated technological culture, found in Jesus
Christ the true redeemer who gave them *as Qom*, renewed hope,
strength and life. Thus, the indigenous church which emerged from a
movement of spiritual awakening in the middle of the twentieth century,
the *Iglesia Evangelica Unida*, reflects a dynamic inculturation of the
Gospel among a people whose world-view is strikingly different from
that of other churches in the Chaco, which simply adopted imported
Western patterns of spirituality and worship. The Qom were able to
distinguish Christ from the culture of the missionaries with the result
that they now believe they have something important to offer to Western
Christians from within their own cultural heritage. Thus, Hugo Diaz, an
indigenous Christian leader, invites Western believers to assist the
church in the Chaco in language which clearly reflects the post-
Christendom context for mission with which this book is concerned:
'We no longer want you to come and teach us the Bible. We want you
to come and read the Bible together with us' (*ibid.*: 179).

For Christians in the Western world who have long thought of themselves as belonging to churches located in a missionary-sending region,
a statement like this presents a considerable challenge. For centuries
mission has involved a movement from the West to the rest of the world
and the traffic that has passed down this busy one-way street has
included personnel, spiritualities and theologies. Consequently,
although Jesus lived in the Near East, 'it was as a religion of Europe
that his message came to the nations of the world and the islands of
the sea' (Pelikan: 1985, 221–2). At the height of European colonial power
Hilaire Belloc could make the provocative claim that 'The Faith is
Europe and Europe is the Faith'. However, as in previous eras, Christ
could not be contained within a single culture and in the course of the
twentieth century it became ever clearer that he is indeed 'The man who
belongs to the world'. In this process, which was the direct outcome,
intentionally or not, of the missionary movement, entirely new dimensions of the grace of God have come to light as more and more peoples
have come to confess Jesus as Lord. Thus, in the voices of Qom believers,
representing millions of Christians in primal cultures throughout the
world, we hear an echo of the One who long ago said: 'He who has an
ear, let him hear *what the Spirit says to the churches*' (Rev. 3:22).

Had the Qom not been converted to Christ, or had their distinctive
world-view been destroyed in the process, 'their contribution to the
complete image of Jesus Christ would still be lacking'. As it is, the Qom

provide us with yet another example of mission as the learning experience of the church. In Willis Horst's words:

> The encounter between Christian missions and the spiritualities of Indigeneous peoples around the world, especially in native American cultures, has forced the church to recognize, and come to terms with, claims to God's revelation in cultures outside the Christian faith . . . We no longer seek to eliminate our own or others' uniqueness, but to celebrate it and to connect each to the whole. Therein lies our hope in a pluralistic world, as we look towards the future when God, according to Ephesians 1:10, will gather all things together in Christ.
>
> (Horst: 2001, 182)

Mission and Pluralism

The story I have been telling so far in this chapter relates to the emergence of *theological* pluralism as the direct outcome of the cross-cultural transmission of the Gospel into new cultures and languages. At the end of his marvellous study of the impact of Jesus on human cultures entitled *Jesus Through The Centuries*, Jaroslav Pelikan observes that as respect for the institutional churches in the Western world has declined, reverence for Jesus has *grown*, and he comments that 'there is more in him than is dreamt of in the philosophy and Christology of the theologians' (Pelikan: 1985, 232–3). This awareness of the limited and partial nature of all human knowledge of Christ is, in fact, a profoundly biblical insight. In one of the best-known passages in the New Testament, the apostle Paul warns of the dangerously misleading nature of narrowly intellectual approaches to the truth and he likens even his own attempts to express the mystery of Christ, enriched as they were by the role he played in mission to the Gentiles, to mere childish prattle in comparison with the final reality (1 Cor. 13:9–13). Commenting on Paul's recognition that our present knowledge of Christ and his grace amounts to little more than a 'poor reflection' of the ultimate reality, the reformer John Calvin observed:

> . . . the knowledge of God, which we now derive from His Word, is undoubtedly reliable and true, and there is nothing muddled, or unintelligible or dark about it; but . . . it falls a long way short of that clear revelation to which we look forward, when we shall see face to face . . . For there is an open and naked revelation of God in the Word (enough

to meet our needs) ... *But how small a share this is of the vision toward which we reach out!* (Calvin: 1960, 282 [emphasis mine])

What Calvin did not appreciate, given his historical and cultural situation, is that the pre-eminent way in which the people of God throughout the centuries reach out towards that ultimate vision of Christ, is through the process of cross-cultural mission. The New Testament itself recognises that, limited though all present human knowledge of God is, the church's understanding of the mystery of Christ can and does increase as Jesus comes to be seen through the lenses supplied by diverse human cultures. Thus, Paul recognises that the mystery of Christ, which had been 'hidden for ages and generations' has been 'disclosed to the saints' as a direct consequence of his own missionary labours among the Gentiles. The apostolic translation of the Gospel among Greeks and Romans has resulted in an enlarged understanding of 'the glorious riches of this mystery, which is Christ in you [Gentiles], the hope of glory' (Col. 1:26–7). Elsewhere he prays for his Gentile converts that they will 'have power, *together with all the saints*, to grasp how wide and long and high and deep is the love of Christ, and to know this love *that surpasses knowledge...*' (Eph. 3:18–19). Clearly, there is a paradox here: the Gospel involves a mystery that transcends all human rational and mystical comprehension, yet as more and more peoples are drawn into the kingdom of grace and add the testimonies and insights that arise from their experience, so the sum total of the church's knowledge of Christ increases and approximates ever more closely to the ultimate reality which will be known only at the last day.

The implications of this for Western theology in particular are immense. We have seen the way in which Christendom claimed exclusive access to truth and grace, with the result that, for more than a thousand years, the normative shape of the Christian religion was determined by its interaction with Western culture. In truth, this entire development obscured the reality of a valid theological pluralism resulting from mission in the East and the South, in ancient traditions of Christianity beyond the sphere of Christendom. It is easy to forget, for example, that the year AD 635 witnessed not only the arrival of Aidan on the island of Lindisfarne to commence the task of evangelising the pagan kingdom of Northumbria, but also saw a missionary bishop from Persia reaching the imperial capital of ancient China, where he began translating the Bible with the support of the emperor. This movement of missionary Christianity eastwards remains a largely untold story, yet its significance is likely to increase in the decades ahead as China moves towards centre stage in the unfolding drama of human history.

However that may be, with the decline of the churches in Europe and the growth of Christianity virtually everywhere else, the realisation grows that the Western phase of Christianity was precisely that – *a phase involving a more or less successful translation of the Gospel among the peoples of the Western world.* This phase has now clearly come to an end and we are witnesses to the emergence of new centres of spiritual and theological vitality as Christians from the southern continents add their insights to the church's total knowledge of the incomparable Christ. In the present transitional stage we are moving *from* a Christendom shaped by the culture of the Western world, *to* a world Christianity which will develop new spiritual and theological insights as the biblical revelation is allowed to interact with the many cultures in which Christ is now confessed as Lord. To ignore this development, withdrawing into a dreamworld in which we imagine that the Christendom model can somehow be revived, is to deny the true significance of mission within God's purpose. Moreover, as Lamin Sanneh says, 'if translatability is the taproot of Christian expansion, then resistance to it by ecclesiastical institutions is like the rebellion of the branches against the tree' (Sanneh: 1990, 30).

This transition is likely to result in changes that we can scarcely imagine at present, but as the missionary-anthropologist Paul Hiebert has observed, the new shape of the Christian movement in the twenty-first century will require that Christians in Europe and North America are open to a major epistemological shift. Theological definitions can no longer be drafted in Rome, Geneva, London or Chicago as though they had some universal and binding validity; rather the world church must become 'an international hermeneutical community' in which Christians from around the globe seek to understand the word of God, dealing with the problems they face in their particular contexts and seeking to develop together a *global* theology 'increasingly freed from the influences of specific human contexts' (Hiebert: 1999, 113).

Toward a Biblical Theology of Religions

If, as I have argued above, all peoples and cultures have valid and important contributions to make to our *theological* understanding of Christ and the Gospel, the question which must now be faced is whether the same principle applies to the *religions* of the world, given that they

61

constitute such a central element of human cultures. Difficult as it undoubtedly is, this question is far from abstract and theoretical in the social and cultural context in which we find ourselves at the beginning of the twenty-first century. In a world which lives after Christendom, and at a time when we witness an historically unprecedented movement of peoples around the globe, religious diversity has become an almost universal fact of life. To refuse to recognise the persistence and strength of other faiths, says Kenneth Cragg, whatever our understanding of the providence at work in this situation, 'is to be at odds with existence' (Cragg: 1968, 65). Young European Christians on holiday in Egypt, Indonesia or India come face to face with *people* belonging to other religious traditions and make the disturbing discovery that they do not necessarily fit the stereotypes of the 'unreached peoples' they have heard about endlessly in Evangelical churches back home. Such travellers are likely to return asking what the term 'unreached' actually means in relation to people who have demonstrated qualities of integrity, hospitality and spirituality that are noticeable by their absence in Western societies. Meantime, older and more experienced Western Christians with solid doctrinal foundations now routinely encounter Muslims and Hindus as colleagues and neighbours and suddenly find themselves wrestling with precisely the kind of issues that so perplexed Henry Martyn in Asia and Persia two centuries earlier. What is more, now as then, this situation exposes the poverty of Western theology when it is put to the test on this missionary frontier. In a postmodern world, ordinary members of Christian congregations in Europe and North America are making the kinds of discovery once limited to cross-cultural missionaries in exotic locations, and, like them, such people are realising that inherited theological traditions forged in the context of a Christian monopoly provide little help when encountering devout adherents of other religions. To ignore this situation, or to respond by merely repeating certain favoured proof-texts which manifestly fail to address the central issues raised by religious pluralism, is to ensure that the tide will continue to withdraw from the churches of the West.

Earlier in this chapter I drew attention to the example of Thomas Aquinas in charting a new way forward for Christian mission in the context of the massive challenge posed by the expansion of Islam in medieval Europe. Aquinas recognised that the inherited model of mission was fundamentally flawed and was never likely to succeed in meeting the challenge posed by Islam. Curtis Chang (to whom I am indebted for this example) traces a parallel between those times and the situation confronting us today, recognising in both what he calls *epochal challenges* – periods when certain major historical and cultural developments call into question 'how the church has travelled the most recent leg of its journey'. For us the challenge is related to the emergence of what we have come to know as *postmodernity*, which, Chang says, 'threatens many paradigms that have long guided the church' (Chang: 2000, 18–19).

The nature and extent of this challenge can be understood in the light of the statement of a well-known contemporary writer and art critic, John Berger: 'Never again will a single story be told as though it is the only one'. The particular story against which Berger is reacting is that told by the philosophers of the Enlightenment, which we have discussed earlier in this book. As we have seen, the confident predictions of the eighteenth-century rationalist thinkers that Western civilisation was the vanguard of a movement which would bring universal human happiness, have been falsified by painful and tragic historical experience. In the resulting atmosphere of disillusion and cynicism, *all* claims to possess absolute truth have become suspect since they are perceived to involve a dangerous arrogance and, all too often, to result in terrible violence. Advocates of over-arching systems of belief which claim to account for the whole of reality, whether these are based on science, political ideology or religion, now stand accused of maintaining the credibility of their beliefs through an ideological selection of facts in which inconvenient evidence (and, tragically, inconvenient *people*) have been eliminated from the story. Such narratives, it is claimed, have always served the interests of the winners in the historical process and enabled them to retain their hold on power and privilege. Postmodernity thus comes to be defined, in Lyotard's now famous phrase, as 'incredulity toward metanarratives' and, conversely, as the affirmation of a radical pluralism. In this situation of epochal change, missionary engagement with people in the real world demands that we ask the question: How can we *retell* the story of the Gospel in such a way as to recognise the validity of many of the concerns of our postmodern contemporaries, while bearing faithful witness to the Christ who leads us beyond the well-documented discontents of the postmodern condition? (See Bauman: 1997)

One of the most urgent requirements of the church at the new frontier of mission constituted by contemporary pluralisation is the creation of a biblical theology of religions which is both faithful and credible. I will return to the quality of biblical faithfulness shortly, but here I want to dwell on the issue of *credibility*. In the globalised world of the twenty-first century, a Christian theology of religions will be credible *only if it deals honestly and accurately with the actual phenomena of religions*. In the past, dogmatic assumptions concerning the nature and behaviour of the populations of the non-Christian world (like those mentioned earlier in relation to the Iberian expansion into the Americas, or indeed, like the assumptions concerning 'savages' which resulted from the dogma of the evolutionary development of the human race) retained credibility as long as only a minority of people experienced cross-cultural encounters which revealed the chasm between dogma and reality. Today, as we have noted above, dogmatic assumptions which take no account of the positive elements in other religions will increasingly be regarded as incredible by a generation well able, through global travel, sociability and the spirit of genuine enquiry, to discover for themselves the dissonance between pulpit pronouncements and the reality of, for example, non-Christian spiritualities.

The insularity of so much Western theology and its failure to take account of the actual phenomena of the religions can be illustrated by a famous encounter between Karl Barth and the Indian Christian theologian, D.T. Niles. Barth was, of course, well known for his hostility toward the religions that he regarded as purely human inventions which prevented people from encountering the living God, revealed in Jesus Christ. Overhearing Barth declare that 'Other religions are just unbelief', the Indian theologian enquired how many Hindus Barth had met. When Barth admitted that he had never actually met a Hindu, Niles pressed his questioning further: 'How then do you know that Hinduism is un-belief?' To this question Barth replied: '*A priori.*' Niles recorded that he smiled and turned away.

How, one wonders, would Karl Barth have responded to an Indian theist like Devedranath Tagore? Rejecting Indian monism, he viewed the world, not as part of *maya*, but as the work of a wise and loving creator. It is indeed difficult to imagine a more beautiful statement of the evidence for God provided by the design of the natural world than the following:

> I saw that the child, as soon as born, drinks at its mother's breasts. Who taught it to do this? He alone who gave it life. Again, who put love into the mother's heart? Who but He that put milk into her breast? He is the God that knows all our wants, whose rule the universe obeys.

> (Richards: 1985, 26)

With regard to his own spiritual search, Tagore could say, 'I had not known how boundless was His mercy. The craving I had felt when seeking for Him increased a hundredfold now that I have found Him' (*ibid.*: 28). In the next generation, Devendranath's youngest son, Rabindranath Tagore, produced a volume of mystical poetry addressing the personal God whom he elsewhere called the 'Life of my life':

> Let only that little be left of me whereby I may name thee my all.
> Let only that little be left of my will whereby I may feel thee on every side, and come to thee in everything, and offer to thee my love every moment.
> Let only that little be left of me whereby I may never hide from thee.
> Let only that little of my fetters be left whereby I am bound to thy will, and thy purpose is carried out in my life – and that is the fetter of thy love.
>
> (Tagore: 1986, 26–7)

It would not be difficult to multiply examples of this kind from across the religious traditions. Constance Padwick spent years travelling in Muslim countries and amassed an extraordinary collection of popular devotional manuals containing prayers which breathe the spirit of devotion and longing for fellowship with God. Here is an example:

> O God, some sought from Thee this world and Thou gavest it to them. And others sought from Thee the next world and Thou didst satisfy them. But I ask Thee neither for this world nor for the next, but only for the increase of love for Thee in my heart. (Padwick: 1961, 136)

This is what I mean by the *phenomena* of religions. I do not intend to suggest that this is the whole picture, far from it. Indeed, there is obvious truth in Barth's assessment of human religion as 'unbelief' and he had first-hand experience of the manner in which religion is capable of aligning itself with demonic powers and sanctifying acts that are unspeakably evil. This dark side of religion must not be ignored or edited out of the picture, but neither should it be taken for the *whole* picture. The statements quoted above expressing profound longing for the knowledge of God and his grace are not unusual and they give rise to legitimate theological questions which demand from Christians a biblically based response. What is the source and status of such religious experience? How is such spirituality to be related to Christ and the Gospel? What kinds of challenge arise for the largely cerebral Christianity of the West from the encounter with mystical, experiential traditions of this kind? The questions go on multiplying, but these are sufficient to give us the measure of the problem and they serve to underline the wisdom of Kenneth Cragg's response: 'Can we at once confess the dimensions of our problem, *as being too big for our theology, but not for our faith?*' (Cragg: 1968, 83 [emphasis mine]).

What happens when we bring such questions to the Bible? I have said that we need a theology of religions that is both relevant and *faithful.* However, faithfulness does not mean merely treading well-worn paths of interpretation and continuing to operate within the parameters set by a careful and limited selection of texts that are guaranteed to supply the answers we want to hear. On the contrary, faithfulness demands *an openness to the total witness of the Bible and a recognition that the Holy Spirit may have more to teach us on these issues than we have yet been able to receive.* As we have seen throughout this study, inherited cultural and intellectual traditions create particular mindsets which come to limit what the Bible is allowed to say to us. As Douglas John Hall observes, most discussions of mission in our pluralist context are skewed 'by the Constantinian assumptions at work in the minds of the participants' with the result that entrenched traditions of interpretation predetermine answers even before the questions have been defined (Hall: 1998, 67). We recall here that at the beginning of the modern missionary movement William Carey had to break a theological log-jam before the apostolic summons to mission could be heard and obeyed within the Protestant tradition with which he was associated. Now, at the opposite end of the historical phase initiated by Carey's boldness and insight, we are required to recognise the blind spots which may need to be overcome in our reading of the Bible at the new frontiers of mission today.

Where might such blind spots be located? In the previous chapter we saw how the prophets of ancient Israel dealt with 'religion', critiquing *both* the traditions of their own people when these degenerated into dead, ideological forms at odds with the covenant faith revealed to Moses, *and* the imperial faith of Babylon which sanctified raw power and set up monstrous idols in the place of the living God. We will return to this critical, biblical tradition later in this book and will notice how it is continued and developed in the light of Christ in the book of Revelation. The fact is that this searching biblical evaluation of human religions closely parallels the modern, secular critique found in the work of such thinkers as Ludwig Feuerbach, Karl Marx and Sigmund Freud. Consequently, we should not reject out of hand the modern awareness than religion can involve human projections and that it frequently serves vested interests and prevents necessary change and reform within society. Precisely such perspectives inform the preaching of Israel's greatest prophets, so that the secular critics of religion are less a threat to faith than a challenge to faithfulness and their work should drive Christians back to their own source of authority in the scriptures.

This was, as we have seen, the focal point of Karl Barth's theology of religions. Having experienced at first hand a highly ideological form of religion that co-opted Christ into the service of a racist and militaristic nationalism, Barth recognised the validity of much of the modern criticism of religion. However, he went beyond this by confessing the truthfulness of the biblical witness concerning the *demonic* elements in religion and treated this perspective with utter seriousness. This is a crucial strand in the biblical treatment of human religion and there is a real danger today that, in the context of radical pluralism, it can be ignored and suppressed. Faithfulness to the witness of scripture demands that we recognise that it is often the most pious and devout of people who run the risk 'of being further removed from God' than anyone else (Bosch: 1977, 183).

Having said this, we should pay equal attention to another, contrasting theme that runs through the biblical narratives. According to the psalmist, God answers the prayers of 'all who call on him in truth' (Psalm 145:18). It seems impossible to limit this promise to the prayers of Israel or the church because it occurs in a context in which it is repeatedly insisted that the Lord 'has compassion on *all* he has made' and 'watches over *all* who love him'. The biblical universalism of this psalm is clear in relation to the creator's providential care for all peoples, but it must also extend to his merciful response to those same people whenever they seek his grace. This text enables us to recognise the significance of the appearance of 'godly pagans' in the biblical narratives, people like Melchizedek, Abimelech and Jethro, among many others, whose surprising piety and great wisdom punctuate the story again and again. Indeed, in the case of Nebuchadnezzar in Daniel 4, we have an example of a pagan who receives direct divine revelation by means of a dream which results in his conversion and public confession of the glory and grace of the living God. This is an extraordinary narrative that simply explodes with meaning in relation to this discussion, yet few Old Testament commentators seem to recognise its missiological significance.

Here, I suggest, is the 'blind spot' which prevents us from recognising the generosity and freedom of divine grace as this is displayed within the biblical narrative. Consequently, although the questions we raised above concerning the religions can be answered faithfully from within the biblical tradition, this task awaits theologians and biblical commentators with the insight, courage and devotion to Christian mission that have, alas, been rare within the guilds of scholarship operating within a Christendom framework.

5

A Biblical Model:
Peter in the House of Cornelius

In the previous chapter I suggested that the supreme model for the cross-cultural transmission of the Gospel of Jesus Christ is to be found within the pages of the New Testament. In other words, the struggle we are engaged in at the new frontiers of mission in the twenty-first century is not something unique to our times, but is a re-run of the challenging and dangerous missionary task with which the apostles of Christ were themselves familiar. For them, as for us, the spiritual and theological issues raised by the demands of the cross-cultural translation of the Gospel involved an immense struggle, evidence of which is to be found throughout the New Testament.

The precise nature of the task confronting the early believers was determined by a cultural and historical context in which *Jewish* believers faced the challenge of making the message of Jesus the Messiah intelligible to *Gentile* pagans. The term 'Messiah' actually takes us straight to the heart of the theological and religious issues involved in this first great missionary movement across cultures, since, precious as it was to Jews, *it communicated nothing to their receptors in the Graeco-Roman world*. In this situation translation involved devising a new Christology in which this familiar Jewish title became a proper name, now explained and applied by the addition of a word immediately recognised in the Gentile world, the ambiguous term 'Lord'. The New Testament thus charts a progression in which the confession 'Jesus *is* Messiah' is expanded in the wider world shaped by Roman concepts, to become 'Jesus Christ (Messiah) *is Lord*'.

Not surprisingly, the book of Acts bears clear witness to the controversial nature of this project and even though the 'Council of Jerusalem' (Acts 15) granted formal approval to cultural pluralism within the church, considerable resistance to it persisted in practice, as the sharp conflicts and disagreements reflected in the Pauline correspondence indicate. If there is a single point in the narrative of the book of Acts at which the issues arising in the practice of cross-cultural mission are brought into particularly clear focus, it is in the story of the encounter between the apostle Peter and the Roman centurion, Cornelius. I propose therefore to examine the four sections, or scenes, which constitute this narrative in some detail, noting its relevance to the discussion of pluralism in the previous chapter.

Scene One: In the House of a Gentile God-Seeker (Acts 10:1–8)

The opening verses plunge us straight into the heart of the central issues with which we are concerned here. Cornelius is introduced as a Roman soldier of high rank who, together with all his family, is 'devout and God-fearing'. He is described as being 'generous' to the poor and needy, and as someone who prayed to God 'regularly' (10:1–2). The phrases are piled one upon another to drive home the point that this man is truly godly and pious. It is taken for granted that his prayers are directed to the living God and the description carefully draws our attention to the harmony between religion and ethics in his life. What is more, Cornelius is clearly not an isolated individual since, as the subsequent narrative indicates, he stands as leader and representative of a large group of people (10:27). This group includes the members of his extended family who clearly share his piety, and there are indications that other Roman soldiers are devout seekers after God (10:7). John Calvin once again demonstrates his greatness as a biblical commentator in his treatment of this narrative and it is worth quoting him at some length:

> But if this man, who was inspired by such a frail and rudimentary faith, was such a splendid mirror of uprightness and sanctity, when so many obstacles confronted him, ought we not to be ashamed, we who wish to be considered Christian teachers, and are so very cold in the exercises of piety? If a small spark of faith had such a great effect on him, what ought the full splendour of knowledge be bringing about in us? *But as we boast loud-mouthed of Christ, how far removed most of us are from the example of this holy man, so that there is apparent scarcely a tiny shadow of the virtues which he had in abundance.*
>
> (Calvin: 1965, 286 [emphasis mine])

Here, as at many points throughout this narrative, there is a parallel with the story of Jonah in the Old Testament. In both accounts reluctant missionaries discover genuine piety in unexpected places and are put to shame by the manner in which people from outside the covenant take God and his word with absolute seriousness.

No one familiar with the Christian mission will be surprised by the positive manner in which pagan piety is described in these texts because people like Cornelius appear repeatedly in the history of mission. Timothy Richard, a Baptist who spent forty-five years working in China, describes how, early in his missionary career, he encountered a devout man who showed him a spotlessly clean inner room in his house which had provided a sanctuary in which he had worshipped God every day of his life. On reading a hymn book the missionary had with him, the man said of a Christian song describing the transient nature of the world, 'This hymn is ours'. Richard found himself rendered speechless by this encounter and wrote later, 'I was dumb and felt that his religious experience was not only much earlier than mine, but possessed a depth which astonished me' (Cracknell: 1995, 122).

Sometimes entire peoples have revealed a God-fearing piety of this kind. The Karen who live in what is now Myanmar, possessed traditions concerning a supreme deity whom they described as the 'real God', traditions that went back to ancient times and had been carefully preserved throughout the ages. Long before Christian missionaries arrived on the scene, the Karen had acknowledged this creator-God whom they called *Y'Wa*, who, as local teacher-prophets devoted to him constantly reminded them, was alone worthy of love and worship. Children were taught to revere this holy name and tribal songs made it clear that any careless mention of *Y'Wa* caused him to withdraw further than ever from the Karen. In practice, the people feared many lesser spiritual powers and, aware of a rupture between themselves and *Y'Wa*, they lived in hope and expectation that a way would eventually be revealed to restored fellowship with the true God. From generation to generation these extraordinary traditions were passed on, largely through stories and songs like the following:

> At the appointed season *Y'Wa* will come.
>> Dead trees will blossom and flower,
>> Mouldering trees will blossom and bloom again.
> *Y'Wa* will come and be the great *Thau-thee* [sacred mountain]
> Let us ascend and worship.

The missionary-anthropologist who recorded these traditions (and many others like them among primal peoples scattered across Asia) comments that the pre-Christian Karen seem to have possessed a sense of reverence and spiritual hunger which 'probably exceeded that of history's average Jew or Christian'. The Karen were 'poised like an 800,000–member welcoming party, ready for the first unsuspecting missionary who approached them with a Bible and a message of deliverance from God' (Richardson: 1981, 81–3).

The question might be asked at this point as to whether we can anticipate the discovery of this kind of piety in the post-Christian culture with which we are concerned in this book. It is one thing to recognise that pre-existing beliefs among primal peoples offer a point of contact for the message of the Gospel, but surely no Cornelius-like piety will emerge from the wastelands of the deeply secularised culture we have described in earlier chapters. The presumption tends to be that where the message of the cross has been pushed to the margins of culture and people have consciously turned away from faith, then the very foundations of belief will have been destroyed and even the rumours of God will fade away. But what if the quest for spiritual reality and the longing for answers to the ultimate issues concerning life and death constitute an ineradicable aspect of what it means to be human? And what if the loss of privilege and power proves to be the means of liberation for the churches in the West, creating a situation in which they can recover credibility among people who *are* asking Cornelius-like questions?

The Czech theologian, Jan Milic Lochman describes how, during the Communist domination of Eastern Europe, the removal of the traditional privileges from the churches created a new context in which, to the surprise of many, there were 'positive spiritual possibilities'. In a post-Christendom situation in which atheism had become the official creed, questions concerning God were officially suppressed, and yet precisely in that context they kept resurfacing and came to be discussed with an urgency and honesty previously unknown. Lochman comments,

> Far from vanishing from the range of vital human interests, this officially silenced theme of God became for some, for the first time, in the very midst of attempts to suppress it officially, an even more 'question-able' theme . . . Indeed, at the very moment when it lost the official protection of society, just when it became culturally displaced and 'homeless' in virtue of the shattering of all its internal and external

ideological self-evidence, *the theme of God took on fresh actuality and credibility.* (Lochman: 1988, 47 [emphasis mine])

Can we anticipate a similar resurgence of interest in the ultimate existential questions in the post-Christian Western world? Throughout the twentieth century, psychologists and social scientists have documented a looming crisis, which may indeed provide the fertile soil within which the very questions asked by Roman pagans in the first century re-emerge. It should not surprise us that the cinemas, theatres, bookshops and art galleries of Europe and North America are full of 'signals of transcendence' because the wastelands of modernity are ultimately as unsatisfying to human beings today as was the idolatry and materialism of the Roman empire to the centurion stationed at Caesarea in the first century. Douglas Coupland, having described the sheer boredom of life for a generation that feels it has arrived *after* the ages of faith, and so lives, to use the title of one of his books, *Life After God*, makes this confession:

Now – here is my secret:

I tell it to you with an openness of heart that I doubt I shall ever achieve again, so I pray that you are in a quiet room as you hear these words. My secret is that I need God – that I am sick and can no longer make it alone. I need God to help me give, because I no longer seem capable of giving; to help me be kind, as I no longer seem capable of kindness; to help me love, as I seem beyond being able to love.

(Coupland: 1994, 359)

No one can read a statement like this without realising that the real problem for the Christian mission in the modern West is not the absence of spiritual hunger within the postmodern generation, *but rather the church's failure to recognise the existence and significance of this quest on the part of thousands of people beyond its doors. Even where such recognition does occur there is often a refusal to respond on the terms set by the searchers, rather than those dictated by existing ecclesiastical traditions and structures.*

But to return to Cornelius! The first scene closes with a direct divine response to this Gentile God-seeker (10:3–6). Does God answer the prayers of devout people who have never heard the Gospel? Is divine revelation given to such people in the absence of missionaries? The angel sent to this Roman centurion leaves little room for doubt about the answers to such questions: *'Your prayers and gifts to the poor have come up as a remembrance before God*. Later in the narrative, in a direct reference to this statement, Peter is heard confessing that he has made the revolutionary discovery that God 'does not show favouritism but accepts men *from every nation who fear him and do what is right*' (10:34–5). However, with the assurance granted to the Gentile seeker there also comes an instruction to send messengers to Joppa to bring back a man who can point to the Christ in whom all such human longings and desires find their true fulfilment. Sadly, it is at this point that the problems begin!

Scene Two: The Call of Peter to Cross-cultural Mission (10:9–23)

The literary structure of the first two scenes is similar; in both the prayer of the central character leads on to a vision, which is then followed by a special divine revelation. However, there is also a contrast between Cornelius, who is open, responsive and obedient to the divine word, and Peter, whose reaction is characterised by confusion, resistance and rebellion. The contrast is striking and disturbing; the man without the Bible is humbly obedient to the light given to him, while the one with all the privileges, who in this case has actually walked with the incarnate Word of God, resists further light and will not budge from an inherited theological position.

It is important to consider carefully the nature of the obstacles that initially prevented Peter from following the call of the missionary Christ. He has a vision in which a sheet comes down from heaven containing both clean and unclean animals, which he is then commanded to 'Kill and eat'. His reaction is a very strong one, something like the ringing statement: '*Never, Lord!* For not once in my life have I ever eaten anything unclean' (10:14). Peter has always understood his dietary behaviour to reflect the divine will since it was based on what seemed to be special revelation. The dietary laws were not a merely human construction designed to provide ethnic distinctiveness to the Jewish people, but were an expression of *holiness*. It is this perspective which explains the strength of Peter's reaction and his seeming irreverence in resisting the voice from heaven. He is, we might say, arguing for God against God. Peter's resistance to the divine command is long and vigorous, so that even after the instruction has been issued and declined three times he is still left 'wondering about the meaning of the vision' (10:17).

What is in fact happening here is that the apostle is making the painful discovery that *things he has always regarded as unchanging absolutes were in fact, in the light of Jesus Christ, culturally relative*. In a missionary context the church will always find itself involved in the struggle to distinguish biblical absolutes from culturally conditioned beliefs and practices. The great Puritan preacher Richard Sibbes once accused his contemporaries of 'making more sins than God has made' and long-established theological traditions are always in danger of limiting Christian freedom by an unwarranted expansion of beliefs and practices classified as absolutes. Put another way, mission involves the discovery that *our* faith and theology have been conditioned by culture to a far greater extent than we had ever realised. Cultural conditioning is not something that happens only to other people, we too carry cultural baggage which needs to be declared 'excess' and left behind when we seek to share Christ with others.

The meaning of the vision is made clear not by further words, but by a knock on the door and a face-to-face encounter with spiritually hungry Gentiles (10:21). Eugene Peterson brilliantly paraphrases the text at this point: 'As Peter, puzzled, sat there trying to figure out what it all meant, the men sent by Cornelius showed up' (Peterson: 1993, 304). What appeared contradictory and confusing when considered at an abstract, theoretical level, began to make sense when dealing with living people who testified that they had been hearing words from God. Even then the apostle remained in a state of shock and, in a detail that surely introduces an element of humour into the narrative, he asks his visitors if *they* know what is going on. (10:21) At the conclusion of this scene Peter takes a momentous step which, insignificant though it may appear to modern readers, was in reality the beginning of a revolution: he 'invited the men into the house *to be his guests*' (10:23).

We can surely conclude that Peter is here in the throes of what we have called a paradigm change. He stands, so to speak, on the fault line between two eras and feels the foundations moving beneath him. He is conscious of being led forward, yet the way ahead and the full consequences of his own actions, remain unclear. Here is a man, to revert to terminology used earlier, in a liminal state, discovering that inherited patterns of obedience and holiness have grown old, yet groping toward the newer, deeper understanding which is now being revealed to him. At the core of this struggle are what has been called 'the larger meaning of Christ' and the implications of this for the life and fellowship of the people of God.

Scene Three: Cross-cultural Missionary Witness in Practice (10:24–48)

If Peter's invitation to Gentiles to enter his house as welcome guests is the beginning of a revolution at the level of the new *fellowship* created by Christ, his journey to Caesarea with them represents the transformation of *mission* in line with the final words of the risen Jesus. Spectacular though the growth of the church had been up to this point, the new community remained ethnically homogenous and had barely spread beyond Judea and Samaria. Consequently, Peter's willingness, despite continuing fears and uncertainty, to move on to Gentile territory as the bearer of the good news of the Gospel, was a momentous development because it established the apostolic norm for Christian mission as involving centrifugal movements from the centre towards the peripheries. This may seem to be one small step for Peter, but it was a giant leap for the church of Jesus Christ.

Once in Cornelius' house, Peter does a number of things. First, he is obliged to *disabuse his hearers of false ideas they may entertain concerning himself.* The Roman soldier greeted him with reverence, falling on his knees in humility and gratitude before this representative of the living God. Peter responds with words that appear harsh: 'Stand up, I am only a man myself' (10:26). It may be that the centurion's intention was merely to show respect for a teacher in a manner that was normal within his culture and his action may have involved nothing sinister within his own framework of understanding. Yet Peter will take no risks here, knowing that in this pagan culture stories of the descent of the gods in human form were widespread. Indeed, a few chapters later in this very book, Paul and Barnabas are horrified to discover themselves being revered as divinities by local people who interpreted their actions within the framework of traditional myths that told of the appearance of the gods on earth in the form of human beings (14:11ff).

Actually, the importance of Peter's ringing statement as to his essential *humanity* can hardly be overstressed. The term 'missionary' has often been understood by peoples in the non-Western world in a manner that conferred almost godlike status on those thus identified. Missionaries who have gone from the West to traditional cultures shaped by oral traditions and simple technologies have often seemed to be semi-divine beings in the eyes of their receptors. Their extraordinary wealth and the power they wielded through Western science and medicine endowed them with abilities that seemed nothing less than miraculous.

Indeed, the founder of a mission working in the Sahel region of Africa could claim that he and his colleagues had gone among the peoples of the Sudan 'as demi-gods' with a responsibility to act *in loco parentis* to 'backward peoples' (Boer: 1984,44–5). And if this imbalance in wealth and resources constituted a problem for missionary communication in the nineteenth and twentieth centuries, it is enormously magnified today in the era of consumerism and globalisation. We shall return to this subject in the next chapter, but we must ask ourselves at this point how rich Christians can claim, like Peter, that they are 'only human' when speaking to people who face an unending daily struggle to find food enough to keep their children alive.

One is reminded of the story of a visit that Thomas Aquinas is said to have made to the Pope as he was counting a huge pile of gold and silver coins. 'You see, Thomas' the Pope is reported to have said, 'the successor of St Peter can no longer say "Silver and gold have I none".' Aquinas replied: 'True, Holy Father, but neither can he say to lame men, "Rise up and walk"!' While this anecdote might once have served as Protestant propaganda against the Roman church it now takes us close to the roots of the crisis facing Western Christianity and its mission in general since, in a world divided between the absolute poor and the incredibly rich, mission *from* the West is almost unavoidably an enterprise conducted by people who come from the latter to the former. Western missionaries, however they may be perceived at home, have resources which enable them to travel freely around the globe, so that from the viewpoint of the world's poor and suffering peoples they appear to inhabit an island of prosperity in a sea of poverty (Bonk: 1989, 175). What will be required of them if they are to sound credible when claiming with Peter, 'I am only a man myself'?

There is a further, even more challenging, question. Granted that the designation 'missionary' has long been open to misunderstanding, is it also the case that the more basic term 'Christian' now carries meanings remote from its original significance? For example, how do those contemporary seekers after spiritual reality to whom reference has already been made, understand this term? Alas, Christians are too often perceived as people who have difficulty acting as normal human beings since their religion appears to remove them to a plane remote from the lives lived by ordinary mortals. Beyond the level of the basic courtesies of life, Christians frequently seem to restrict social contacts to those who share their religious world-view and an entire sub-culture exists to make just this kind of enclosed life possible. Douglas Coupland, whom we met earlier, reflects on the impression made upon him by the encounter with people who 'seemed to be talking about Jesus nonstop'. While the existence of Jesus was obviously real for them, he says, 'I was cut off from their experience in a way that was never connectable' (Coupland: 1994, 183). In a cultural and historical context like this, the credibility of the church will depend increasingly on the extent to which Christians can demonstrate that their faith holds both the promise and the dynamic to create human beings able to live full and meaningful lives and unafraid of facing reality.

The second action Peter takes in this situation is to *disabuse himself of mistaken ideas he has had concerning his hearers.* This is the reverse side of the coin. With wonderful honesty the apostle admits that only through the irresistible leading of the Holy Spirit has he been able to make the changes in thought and practice that make it possible for him to be standing before the audience he now confronts in the house of Cornelius. 'You know perfectly well,' Peter says (I paraphrase the apostle's words), 'that twenty-four hours ago I would never have entered this building.' In a statement that indicates the manner in which preconceived assumptions are here simply falling away, he acknowledges that God has revealed that '*I should not call any man impure or unclean*' (10:28). In the *practice* of mission the full meaning of the puzzling vision of the sheet let down from heaven is now becoming clear as the apostle realises that the abrogation of the dietary laws pointed toward the far greater truth that Christ has opened the kingdom of heaven to all humankind. In this process Peter's Jewish preconceptions concerning the Gentiles have been falsified; they are not 'impure or unclean' as the standard, stereotyped image had suggested, but rather display an astonishing openness and receptivity to God. Peter's language indicates that he is literally learning on his feet: '*I now realise* how true it is that God does not show favouritism but accepts men from every nation who fear him and do what is right' (10:34).

In the previous chapter we have observed the ways in which mission has repeatedly proved to be 'the learning experience of the church'. What this narrative indicates is that this pattern can be traced back to the beginning, so that we discover here a principle that belongs to the very essence of biblical Christianity. In crossing cultures, the missionary teacher *becomes a learner,* the one who is in possession of divine revelation *discovers new truth,* and he who seeks the salvation of others finds himself *converted all over again!* In the process of telling the story of Jesus, the Messiah, to a Gentile audience Peter discovers the fuller, universal implications of his own message with the result that his presentation of the Gospel takes an enlarged and contextualised form that moves beyond affirming the messiahship of Jesus to the announcement that Christ '*is Lord of all*' (10:36).

In this act of proclamation, and in the subsequent recognition that Gentile believers are to be baptised without Jewish cultural demands being laid upon them (10:44–8), Peter already anticipates the outcome of the Council of Jerusalem. Yet again we witness here a massive change, because at this point the pre-existing Jewish model of the expansion of the religious community by means of *proselytisation* is being set aside in favour of a new model of mission involving *conversion*. The former practice sought to guarantee that new adherents adopted the patterns of belief and behaviour already established as normative within the believing community and to this end they were circumcised, immersed in water and systematically instructed in the Law of Moses. They became, to all appearances, Jewish. But when, following the outpouring of the Holy Spirit on his Gentile hearers, Peter proceeds immediately to baptise Gentiles as believers in Jesus, he deliberately bypasses the normal cultural barriers thrown up to preserve the internal purity of the covenant community and accepts Cornelius and his friends as Roman followers of Jesus of Nazareth. Conversion does not involve the abandonment of one's previous cultural identity, but a turning toward Jesus Christ *from within it*. This is an astonishing move which makes possible a variety of forms of Christianity, each at home within its own cultural setting and able to bring its own treasures of wisdom and knowledge to the feet of the crucified Lord. As a result, Christianity is from its inception characterised by a cultural pluralism which permits the formation of churches reflecting human diversity and grants recognition to the insights into the mystery of Christ derived from the experience of faith in him within those various contexts. This really was an extraordinary breakthrough and we shall return to it when we discuss the practice of mission at the new frontiers at the end of this book.

Scene Four: Apologetic for New Advance (11:1–8)

The final scene is a dismal one. Peter returns to Jerusalem, to the 'mother church', to find himself the object of suspicion and severe criticism. The 'circumcised believers', jealous of those very barriers which the missionary had ignored in establishing a Gentile-convert congregation, now attack him for entering into table fellowship with 'uncircumcised men' (11:2). The glories of the grace of God in the lives of Cornelius and his many friends are not even on the agenda of this meeting, eclipsed by the more urgent business of ensuring the continued orthodoxy of the missionary through a curbing of his alarming tendency toward innovation and irregularity.

Alas, even a superficial acquaintance with missionary history will be enough to convince us that this picture is accurate and realistic. Peter's experience has been repeated again and again in the history of the cross-cultural transmission of the faith as those who have broken new ground for the sake of Christ have found themselves carpeted by the guardians of the orthodox faith. Both the Roman Catholic Matteo Ricci, seeking to incarnate the message of Christ in the context of Chinese culture and religion, and the pioneering Protestant missionary to India, Bartholomew Ziegenbalg, struggling to gain a sympathetic and accurate understanding of Hinduism, experienced the pain of negative, critical reactions from home churches convinced that their mono-cultural theologies had defined orthodox belief for all times and all places. Ziegenbalg arrived in South India in 1706 and, starting from a position close to zero, attempted to understand the religion of his receptors by the careful study of original sources. In modern terms his grasp of Hinduism was never more than elementary, but he found himself reflecting on how much further Indians seemed to have progressed in the knowledge of God than the pagans of ancient Rome. After conversing with Hindu holy men, Ziegenbalg observed that while God was the *object* of the Christian's faith, he was at least the *subject* of the Hindu's searching. Here was a Petrine experience in Asia in which preconceived European ideas concerning heathen darkness were challenged by the discovery of unexpected levels of Hindu piety. But when Ziegenbalg sent home a manuscript giving expression to these thoughts, believing that his findings would increase the understanding of European Christians, he was to receive a severe rebuff. The director of the Halle Mission replied that German believers had sent Ziegenbalg to India 'to extricate heathenism, not to spread heathenish nonsense in Europe'.

A century later, William Carey and his colleagues in Bengal had exactly the same experience when their determination to adopt a *conversionist* model of mission drew fierce critical comment from England. The Serampore missionaries defined their aims in terms of the creation of an Indian church at home in a Hindu culture and, to that end, they used their famous printing press to publish not only Carey's translations of the Bible, but new editions of the Hindu epics, the Mahabarata and the Ramayana, together with translations of the works of Confucius. Only thus, Carey believed, could a church emerge on the sub-continent which would be both rooted in the Christian scriptures and closely related to Indian cultural traditions. Yet there were constant rumblings from England that the funds provided for a Baptist press had not been intended to promote the circulation of pagan literature. 'I am sorry,' wrote Joshua Marshman, 'that some of my acquaintance in England are not ready to lend a helping hand in the work of the mission, but still question whether it be more than a project of men'.

At this point what is important is the manner in which those involved in breaking new ground for the Gospel react to such criticism. Given the fact that the church in the West now finds itself in a context in which cross-cultural mission must become its highest priority, this is very far from being an academic question. The very survival of Christianity in Europe and America depends upon the emergence of men and women able to think new thoughts and devise new strategies at the real frontiers of mission today. But such people, whether innovative church-planting missionaries or Christian intellectuals seeking to move beyond timeworn habits of thought in order to rethink the relationship of Christianity and Western culture from the perspective of mission, are likely to face misunderstanding, criticism and serious opposition. Like Peter the apostle and generations of pioneering, Spirit-led missionaries before them, those who are ready to confront the challenge posed by Western culture must not be surprised if they are accused of unorthodoxy, even heresy, or are verbally attacked by people who interpret their missionary vision as something liable to undermine the moral purity and integrity of the church of Jesus Christ. In such situations, we do well to take careful note of Peter's response to his critics in Jerusalem in the first century.

What Peter does is simply to explain 'everything to them precisely as it happened' (11:4). He neither takes personal offence nor leaps to his own defence, but recalls, with careful attention to each detail, the steps in his own recent, surprising pilgrimage. Throughout this account he stresses both his own instinctive opposition to the actions he was called to take (11:8) and the sovereign and gracious activity of the Holy Spirit in the unfolding drama (11:12,15–16). In other words, Peter has not forgotten that he previously occupied precisely the same theological ground as that of his accusers. Unlike him, they have not had the advantage of crossing the cultural chasm between Jews and Gentiles and discovering that quite new theological questions arise on the other side of the barricades. Consequently, Peter has something positive to share with his brothers, so that his account avoids self-righteous justification and is marked by a tone of humble *testimony*. At the same time, the crucial and clinching component in this account concerns the activity of the Holy Spirit and the conclusion that, whatever his own natural inclinations may have been, it proved impossible to be found in opposition to God (11:17). It is this statement that finally wins over the doubters who now confess, with a significant indication of lingering suspicions, 'So then, God has *even granted Gentiles* repentance unto life' (11:18).

I propose that Peter is here a model for Christians engaged in mission who discover themselves to be misunderstood and unjustly criticised. He neither concedes the argument to his conservative critics, nor dismisses them as reactionaries who do not merit his time. Peter, like Paul at a later point in the New Testament, will not deny the revelatory nature of the lessons he has learned in mission, but neither does he make this a pretext for dividing the church by forming a sect defined by an anti-Jewish stance. The reason for this is clear: the very principle of cultural plurality which is established by this narrative, a principle which validates the emergence of a distinctively Hellenistic form of Christianity, also justifies the continuation of a *Jewish* church and makes imperative the struggle to maintain the overall unity of Christians, whatever their ethnic identity, within the one body of Jesus Christ. Missionaries, evangelists and theologians who seek to break new ground at the frontiers of cultures and religions must also seek to cope with the tension between the new and the old, encouraging the emergence of fresh forms of the church while remaining in fraternal dialogue with the congregations from which they have come, always seeking to remind brothers and sisters at both ends of this spectrum of their primary and overarching identity as members of the new humankind brought into existence by the redemptive love of God revealed in Christ.

6

Finding the New Frontiers:
(3) The Challenge of Globalisation

In the previous chapters our search for the new frontiers of mission has required a return to earlier times in order to find the roots of both contemporary secularisation and pluralisation. Even though the term 'globalisation' is of recent origin, the beginnings of the phenomenon to which it refers are likewise to be found at least five hundred years earlier, at the dawn of the modern period. Thus, early in the sixteenth century, the great Christian humanist scholar Erasmus, reacting to the flood of recent geographical and ethnographic knowledge, observed: *'Europe is a very small part of the world'.*

At some point in the first decade of that century a Dutch artist named Hieronymus Bosch painted a massive triptych with the title *The Garden of Earthly Delights* (pictures 5, 6 and 7). The world depicted in Bosch's art is very different from that known to the intellectuals of the Renaissance, whose anxieties we have discussed earlier in relation to Hans Holbein's *The Ambassadors.* In Bosch's work we confront canvasses populated with some of the strangest and most disturbing images to be found in the history of Western art. Here we enter a world, or perhaps an *underworld,* of dreams and fantasies in which 'forms seem to flicker and change before our eyes' (Gibson: 1973, 9). The three panels of Bosch's greatest masterpiece take us from a Paradise in which human beings exist in perfect harmony with the creator, with each other and with nature; through the reality of the present, fallen existence, where people are hopelessly addicted to carnal pleasures; to a terrifying future, in which human meaning and hope are extinguished in a world with no trace of God, except for the fearsome reality of his abandonment of people to the ultimate outworking of their own depraved choices.

The connection between pictures like this and the phenomenon of globalisation may at first seem remote. However, the links are there and they are important. For example, Bosch's depiction of Paradise reveals his awareness of a world beyond Europe since the precious stones to be seen at the base of the fountain of life, together with the extra-ordinary array of exotic animals, including a giraffe and an elephant, are based upon medieval descriptions of India which originated with the journeys of Alexander the Great (see picture 5). In popular belief the original Garden of Eden was located somewhere in the East, thus creating a significant contrast between the world *beyond* Europe and the artist's own society, dominated, as the central panel depicting fallen humanity suggests, by the search for carnal pleasure and satisfaction.

Even as Bosch was working on this triptych some of his fellow-Christians were discovering the same contrasts between the simplicity and apparent purity of native cultures in the New World, on the one hand, and the greed and idolatry that appeared to drive the *conquista-dores*, on the other. Bartholomé de Las Casas, whom we have already met, arrived in Haiti in 1502 and, after a dramatic experience of con-version which led him to oppose slave-holding, reported that God had made the indigenous peoples 'as open and as innocent as can be imagined'. Native cultures were characterised by a wonderful simplicity and the European observer noticed that, despite their poverty, these people had 'no urge to acquire material possessions'. In the eyes of the invaders the native diet seemed poor and monotonous, but it reminded Las Casas of the exemplary lifestyle of the Desert Fathers! The simplicity of traditional cultures did not imply that these people were intellectually inferior to educated Europeans since the missionary discovered that they possessed 'a lively intelligence' that made them eager to learn and open to the Christian faith. In stark contrast to all this, Las Casas' *A Short Account of the Destruction of the Indies* indicts his fellow-Europeans in language that moves us from Bosch's depiction of Paradise to the horrors of the second and third panels:

> It was upon these gentle lambs, imbued by the Creator with all the qualities we have mentioned, that from the very first day they clapped eyes upon them the Spanish fell like ravening wolves upon the fold, or like tigers and savage lions who have not eaten meat for days.

(Las Casas: 1992 [1542]: 9–11)

When the narrative moves on to describe the Spanish invasion of Cuba, Las Casas reports how a tribal leader, aware of the destruction already visited upon the population of Haiti, attempted to explain the inhuman behaviour of the invaders by identifying the deity worshipped by them. Pointing to a basket full of gold jewellery he said, 'Here is the God of the Christians'. In such ways, says the chronicler, was the reputation and honour of Christ harmed through 'the actions of those "Christians" who have sailed to the Americas' (*ibid.*: 28–9).

Half a century after Las Casas had set foot on the island of Haiti, the first Protestant missionaries arrived in South America, landing on the coast of Brazil in 1556. Jean de Léry, one of a group of fourteen men sent from the Reformed Church in Geneva in response to an appeal for help which had been addressed to John Calvin, wrote an epic account of this mission with the title *History of a Voyage to the Land of Brazil, Otherwise Called America,* in which he described his extraordinary experiences on sea and land, reporting in meticulous detail on both the peoples and the natural wonders of the New World. Four hundred years later, Claude Levi-Strauss stood on the very beach on which the Calvinist missionaries had landed with a copy of the 'breviary of the anthropologist Jean de Léry' in his pocket and paid tribute to the man whose careful ethnography of the Tupinamba indians had been a foundational work for the science of anthropology. Léry's account has been described as a vivid and subtle description of the natural setting of the Tupinamba, which provides us with one of the most detailed and engaging reports 'of how the New World looked while it was indeed still new' (Whatley in Léry: 1990 [1580], xv).

Like Las Casas before him, the French Calvinist Léry was profoundly challenged by the discovery of what he quaintly called 'singular things completely unknown over here'. As Janet Whatley has pointed out, prior to the publication of such careful and sympathetic ethnographies written by missionaries like Léry and Las Casas, the European imagination populated the unknown regions beyond the seas with headless men wearing their eyes on their shoulders and with their ears hanging down to their knees. The discovery of the Americas thus constituted an enormous new fact which exploded such myths and demanded the rethinking of received theological and anthropological assumptions. For the Calvinist Léry the questions were urgent and difficult: where did these entirely new 'others' fit into the biblical narrative? If, as must be the case, they were descended from Adam, how did they get where they are and why were they unaware of the consequence of the Fall in relation to the covering of human nakedness? Furthermore, how should one explain those features of native life and culture which were undeniably admirable, even superior in certain respects to the culture of

Christian Europe? Significantly, Léry did not publish his history until 1578, by which time he had resumed ministry in France and had lived through some of the most terrible religious conflicts of that period. The Saint Bartholomew's Day Massacre had 'flooded across the land in waves of such violence that Frenchmen were to be seen roasting and eating other Frenchmen's hearts', so that when Léry comes to compare the behaviour of European Christians with that of his cannabalistic Tupi friends in the rainforests of Brazil, it is by no means clear who merits the description of 'savages'. Like many another missionary after him, Léry writes of his experiences among the Tupi with undisguised nostalgia: 'I stood there transported with delight', he says of an occasion when he had heard native singing during a traditional religious ceremony. 'Whenever I remember it, my heart trembles, and it seems their voices are still in my ears' (*ibid.*: 143–4). As Léry's translator Janet Whatley observes, such exotic New World cultures resembled the Old World 'in just those aspects that modernity – via the Reformation – would suppress in the name of a purer religion or a more efficient economic structure' (*ibid.*: xxxvi).

The significance of this in relation to the Christian mission at the new frontier of globalisation today is clear: if the origins of that phenomenon are to be traced to the events which historians have come to describe as the 'Columbian Exchange', then Bartholomé de Las Casas and Jean de Léry provide us with models for the practice of mission in a globalised world. At the conclusion of his work, Las Casas explains that he had agreed to publish his account at the insistence of friends in the Spanish court who were deeply concerned for the integrity of the Christian faith and felt compassion for their fellow men in the New World. Las Casas says that his motivation was first, 'to ensure that the teeming millions in the New World, for whose sins Christ gave his life' should have the chance to discover authentic Christianity, and secondly, to provide a prophetic challenge to Spain since he did not wish to see his country 'destroyed as a divine punishment for the sins against the honour of God and the True Faith' (Las Casas: 1992 [1542], 127). Here is a missiology, in all probability influenced by the Christian humanism of Erasmus, which is faithful to Christ and aware of the realities of a changing world; it makes evangelism inseparable from the demands of peace and justice, requires a sensitive appreciation of the positive values in receptor cultures, and articulates a prophetic response to the negative features of the civilisation from which the missionary comes. Moreover, in Bartholomé de Las Casas and Jean de Léry we witness an integrity of Christian *practice* which exemplifies the Erasmian ideal of mission according to which evangelists must offer their hearers a threefold nourishment: holy doctrine, holy living 'and bodily sustenance' (Storrar: 1995, 79).

In returning now to Bosch's painting, I want to consider the central panel, with its extraordinary depiction of human sexual activity (see picture 6). This has prompted considerable scholarly debate, in which opinions as to the meaning of this scene range from those who see it as consistent with medieval Catholic moralising, to those who, suspecting the influence of heretical religious groups, argue that Bosch's garden anticipates 'a sort of universal love-in' (Gibson: 1973, 80). However that issue is resolved, the scene depicted here, located between Paradise and hell, speaks with remarkable power to any culture in which the meaning of life is reduced to the biological functions of the human body. At the centre of the panel a large group of naked men ride a variety of beasts around a pool in which women are bathing and awaiting selection for copulation. Nowhere in Western art has the inability of sex to bear the weight of meaning-creation placed upon it in a godless world been so powerfully depicted as here. In contrast to the first panel, this scene is filled with ceaseless activity, but it is totally devoid of meaning. While Bosch is obviously reflecting his society at the end of the medieval period, his art seems to anticipate the cultural emptiness of much later times, in which one of the few remaining routes to self-transcendence open to secularised people is the experience of orgasm. The central panel of *The Garden of Earthly Delights* is thus extraordinarily relevant to the mission of the church today, reminding us that in cultures devoted to the worship of Mammon and Eros, the greatest challenge is to maintain 'a revolutionary community in a world that often uses sex as a means of momentarily anesthetizing or distracting people from the basic vacuity of their lives' (Hauerwas and Willimon: 1989, 63).

It is, however, when we turn to the third panel that the adumbrations of a secularised and globalised world become most alarming (see picture 7). Here we discover what has been called Bosch's 'spectres and apparitions of hell' depicted by means of grotesque hybrids of birds, beasts and people. This is a phantasmagoric world in which demons control men and evil is dominant everywhere. A huge pair of human ears trundle across the fantastic scene like an infernal battering ram, immolating its victims with a massive knife balanced between the ears. This picture, like Bosch's depictions of hell elsewhere, has no horizon;

there is neither sun nor moon and the only light comes from burning buildings in an underworld where everything seems to be on fire. Indeed, the buildings do more than simply burn; they explode, throwing red and yellow reflections on to the waters below so that these seem to have been turned into blood.

For Hieronymus Bosch and his contemporaries, the message was clear: a life devoted to self-interest and pleasure without reference to God the creator would lead to the chaotic and terrifying existence depicted in this final panel. Bosch's work appears to have been done in the service of Catholic orthodoxy and with the hope that it might stimulate the reform of both church and society. But paintings, like written texts, have meanings which often transcend their original contexts, anticipating larger developments beyond the artist's own times. Commenting on the third panel of *The Garden of Earthly Delights*, art historian and critic John Berger observes that there is 'no continuity between actions' but only 'the clamour of the disparate, fragmentary present'. The picture conveys a feeling of 'spatial delirium' in which human actions have no outcome. Berger invites us to compare this with what we see every night on the TV news bulletins, in which there is 'a comparable incoherence, a comparable wilderness of separate excitements, a similar frenzy'. The globalised culture of our times, he says, lacks a horizon and is characterised by false promises used to justify 'the delinquent and insatiable need to sell'. If we are to survive in a world like this it is imperative that we discover a new horizon which would make possible the recovery of human meaning and genuine *hope*. This will involve 'refusing to accept the absurdity of the world-picture offered to us' and establishing 'pockets of resistance' in which the other two panels of Bosch's remarkable painting 'can be studied by torchlight in the dark' (Berger: 1998, 3–4).

Defining Globalisation

The event which has come to be known throughout the Spanish-speaking countries as the *Conquista* changed the world forever and casts its long shadow down the subsequent centuries. Western thinkers as diverse as Adam Smith and Karl Marx viewed this as the greatest turning point in the whole of human history since it led, on the one hand, to the destruction of the ancient Andean and Mesoamerican civilisations, and on the other hand, marked the beginnings of the growth of Western hegemony. The depopulation of South America was followed by the ravaging of Africa through the trade in human beings transported to the new colonies. In a ten-year period at the end of the eighteenth century over 300,000 African slaves passed through the port of Liverpool en route for the Americas and the total number of Africans sold into slavery has been conservatively estimated at 20 million.

The problem for the Christian mission is that, notwithstanding the prophetic witness of people like Las Casas and Léry, for over four centuries missions inevitably operated within the context of the growth of Western political and economic power around the world. Thus, when the Reformed Christian, Gaspard de Coligny pleaded the cause of Prot-estant missions at the court of the French King Henry II, seeking to open the way for Léry's mission to Brazil, he did so in relation to the *economic* benefits that might accrue to France, arguing that such expeditions could lead to the discovery of 'great riches and other com-modities for the profit of the realm' (Léry: 1990, 4). The king needed no further persuading and offered the mission a gift of 10,000 francs, together with two fine ships, fitted out with artillery. Although mission-aries were frequently critical of the colonial powers and provided their converts with the linguistic, educational and conceptual tools which made possible serious resistance to colonisation, the fact remains that mission accompanied the building of the Western empires and the establishment of patterns of global trading which have shaped the world we inherit today. Now, as a 'global culture creeps with the electricity lines up even the loneliest valleys of the Andes' (Wood: 2000, 18), the nature of the relationship between this globalised, economistic culture and the message of Jesus Christ has become a central issue requiring urgent theological and missiological reflection. As the historian Enrique Dussel has observed, after the fall of the Berlin Wall and the overcoming of tensions between East and West, Christians should now be concerned to face the even greater challenge of a wall that is 'immensely higher and longer', dating back far beyond the twentieth century to the fateful year of 1492, when the foundations were laid for the invisible barrier which separates the rich North from the impoverished South (Dussel: 1990, 42).

At this point, Western Christians concerned to engage in faithful mission at the frontier of globalisation find themselves facing some extremely difficult questions. Is the deepest cause of their spiritual weakness at this frontier to be found in the nature of their relationship with the ideology which has driven this process? Is it the case that the prophetic warnings of people like Bartholomé de Las Casas have been largely ignored within Christendom and that, at the height of 'the age of expanding Europe', the churches entered into a symbiotic relationship with modern culture? After all, it is simply impossible to overlook the fact that the 'great era' of Christian missions occurred as people of European origin extended their political and economic control until it encompassed 84 per cent of the land surface of the globe. The British alone claimed to rule over an empire on which the sun never set and had effective control over 1.5 million square miles. The collapse of the Ottoman empire and its division between Britain, France and Italy pushed the area under European control even higher, peaking around the year 1920. The questions raised by this historical and cultural context concern Western Christianity in general and are not restricted in their application to particular ecclesiastical or theological traditions. Certainly, Evangelicals cannot evade them since, as John Seel has noted, they have reacted to modernity with a strange mixture of intellectual defiance and practical accommodation, carefully maintaining theological orthodoxy 'while simultaneously uncritically accommodating to the tools of modernity whether in marketing the church or mending the soul' (Seel: 1994, 295). For Western Christendom as a whole, then, the question comes to be defined thus: has the acculturation of the churches to a culture shaped by fundamentally materialistic values resulted in the eclipsing of the authentic message of Christ, leaving believers incapable of pointing toward an alternative vision for the future of humankind and the world? This was the view of those nonconformists who, at the high water mark of the modern project, protested at what they perceived to be Christianity's growing syncretism. Tragically, many such people abandoned the faith of their fathers since in their eyes it had degenerated into a religion that, as Jesus had warned, became as useless as salt bereft of the power to arrest corruption.

Take the case of the Victorian intellectual, John Ruskin. He developed a radical critique of the theories of the nineteenth-century political economists, describing their approach as a 'bastard science' which was fundamentally flawed and would prove destructive of human well-being. Far from leading toward universal happiness, as people like Jeremy Bentham, John Stuart Mill and Adam Smith had claimed, this approach reduced people to nothing more than 'covetous machines'. Ruskin predicted that an economic theory divorced from ethical and moral concerns would result in the *material* impoverishment of the weak and poor, and the *spiritual* death of the powerful and wealthy. Beyond that, if every man and woman were released to pursue their own interest without reference to others, this would create structural inequalities between peoples and would lead eventually to the rape and destruction of the natural world. Ruskin argued that Christians would be unable to justify 'the kind of existence to which men are now summoned', involving the mere accumulation of luxuries, if they saw clearly 'the suffering that accompanies it in the world' (Ruskin: 1997 [1862], 228). In other words, the much-vaunted wealth-creation of a small segment of the world's population would lead to the pauperisation of everybody else since the rising standard of living of some people at the heart of the empire could only be achieved at the cost of economic devastation at its periphery. As Ruskin puts it: 'The force of the guinea you have in your pocket depends wholly on the default of the guinea in your neighbour's pocket'.

Beyond this, Ruskin anticipated by more than a century the ecological concerns which are now matters of public debate, insisting in a lyrical passage that 'No air is sweet that is silent' since 'all lovely things are also necessary; – the wild flower by the wayside as well as the tended corn; and the wild birds and creatures of the forest, as well as the tended cattle'. Human beings, Ruskin reminded a biblically literate generation, cannot live by bread only, 'but also by the secret manna; by every wondrous word and unknowable work of God' (*ibid.*: 226). What most appalled Ruskin, however, and contributed towards his personal loss of faith, was the complicity of Christians within the emerging mercantile culture, a compromise that in his eyes amounted to apostasy:

> I know of no previous instance in history of a nation's establishing a systematic disobedience to the first principles of its professed religion. The writings which we (verbally) esteem as divine, not only denounce the love of money as the source of all evil, as an idolatry abhorred of the Deity, but declare mammon service to be the accurate and irreconcilable opposite of God's service: and . . . declare woe to the rich and blessing to the poor. Whereupon we forthwith investigate a science of becoming rich, as the shortest road to national prosperity. (*ibid.*: 341)

Despite such protests, the ideology of market capitalism grew in strength and influence and led eventually to what we have described as a *culture of economism*. That is to say, Western culture came to be dominated by the language and mythology of the market to such an extent that human life is now shaped above all else by the economic dimension. Economic information, from the national budget to the daily rise and fall of stock markets and exchange rates, dominates the news media, while metaphors derived from the business world saturate our language. Institutions, whether hospitals, universities, or churches, are organised and run on strictly economic criteria. Even within mission organisations, an older language of faith and dependence upon God has been reduced to the level of a minority tongue in danger of extinction. Terminology derived from the market has entered all the holy places and left those who still frequent them bereft of the ability to worship 'another king' in the spirit of reverence and awe. Christians may lament this situation, as does John White in a book with the significant title *Money Isn't God – so why is the church worshipping it?*, but the fact remains that the fleeting moments when believers meet to recall their identity as Christians appear increasingly insufficient to sustain faith when living in a culture which defines people every moment of every day as consumers driven by self-interest. This is even more the case when, as White acknowledges, 'the Christian enterprise grows daily less distinguishable from business enterprise' and the Gospel itself is transformed into a marketable product (White: 1993, 61).

If the terminology and imagery of the market has entered the church, the reverse process has also occurred as the business world has adopted the language of faith for its own purposes. This is particularly evident in advertising, where no taboo remains unbroken and no words or symbols are so sacred that they cannot be violated. In 1998 IBM produced a TV advert in which great throngs of humanity were shown going about their work as a caption appeared asking 'Who is everywhere?'. In the background the pop group REM could be heard singing the Nietzschean anthem 'I Am Superman', while IBM proceeded to identify itself with the divine name revealed to Moses as the words 'I AM' were held aloft within the crowd. The divine attributes of omnipotence and omniscience are routinely claimed by multinational business corporations, while advertisements for their products make claims that at other times and in different cultures would appear blasphemous. Coke is 'The Real Thing'; Renault promoted one of its vehicles as embodying 'The Power and The Glory'; while Ericsson cellphones confer the gift of omnipresence on its customers, declaring 'You are everywhere'. Meanwhile, the new priestly class emerging from the mushrooming business schools are trained in their arts by means of best-selling textbooks bearing titles such as *God Wants You To Be Rich* and *Jesus, CEO*. A chapter heading in one of these volumes takes the appropriation of biblical language to its furthest limit, declaring 'The Market's Will Be Done'. It might be possible to laugh off some of this were it not that, as Thomas Frank observes, this co-option of religious language is a clear indication of the manner in which 'the imperatives of Business Man inundated every other way of imagining the world' (Frank: 2001, 5). We have surely here returned to that final, dreadful panel in Bosch's *Garden of Earthly Delights*.

What is more, 'globalisation' refers to *the spread of this economistic culture throughout the world and the attempt to secure its dominance among all peoples everywhere*. The language of 'development' and the division of peoples and regions of the world into those that are 'developed' and 'developing' privileges the world-view of modernity while treating pre-scientific, traditional wisdom as an obstacle to progress. As a result, peoples whose lives have been shaped by non-Western religious world-views are pressured into abandoning socio-economic systems that have proved capable of ensuring their survival for centuries, in favour of an alien economic structure that offers 'short-term benefits to a privileged part of the population' while endangering 'the very survival of the people in the longer term' (Collier and Esteban: 1998, 28). Perhaps it is not surprising that, having plundered the language of religion, the advocates of the gospel of globalisation promote their cause with what often seems to be an evangelical and missionary fervour. Economic liberalisation, the removal of all barriers to trade on terms set by the West, and the abandoning of traditional, alternative approaches which are decreed to be 'uneconomic', all of this is presented as self-evidently positive and true. With the collapse of the Communist world, the global spread of market capitalism has been presented by Western economists, journalists, business leaders and, not least, politicians, as little less than the goal of history and as a beneficent movement that will, if left to act unhindered and unopposed, set humankind free, making them happy, healthy and prosperous. The act of faith required to believe this secular gospel must surely be a supernatural gift, or else an act of unprecedented credulity.

No description of the process of globalisation can be complete which ignores the fact that the apparent triumph of this system has been accompanied by the deployment of huge military forces intended to defend and maintain its dominance. In the year 2000 the United States' Joint Chiefs of Staff published a document entitled 'Joint Vision 2020' in which they declared that their aim was to achieve 'full spectrum dominance' early in the twenty-first century. In practical terms this meant that American forces would possess the ability to defeat any enemy and control any situation anywhere in the world. According to the document, US forces must be able to conduct military operations 'with access to and freedom to operate in all domains – space, sea, land, air and information'. The actions taken by the armed forces of the United States in the wake of the terrible events of 11 September 2001 are entirely consistent with this doctrine and demonstrate how it works in practice. Western economic interests around the world are to be defended by a deployment of military power that is unprecedented in human history, both in its destructive capability and in terms of its enormous cost.

The Human Consequences

The globalisation narrative is usually related by people who, having benefited from the economic and social freedoms this process has made possible, are inclined to eulogise it in positive, if not ecstatic, language. The problem with such accounts is that they conceal the complexities and ambiguities of the globalising world, rendering the negative impact of these developments on the majority of the world's population virtually invisible, while also editing out of the picture the *spiritual* price exacted from its apparent beneficiaries. We thus end up with selective and one-sided accounts of postmodern reality which articulate 'a caste-bound experience of the globals – the vociferous, highly audible and influential, yet rather narrow category of extraterritorials and globe-trotters' (Bauman: 1998, 101). Without denying the positive aspects of globalisation (to which we shall return), what must be insisted upon here is that this process affects people in very different ways, opening up new and undreamed of opportunities for some, while closing down the options for many others, even as it destroys their traditional means of sustaining life and community. Globalisation is not creating, as is often claimed, a homogenised world in which ancient differences and inequalities are being overcome, but is rather resulting in new forms of social and economic division on a worldwide scale.

The diverse results of globalisation can be seen in a specific illus-tration. Naomi Klein has described the emergence of what she calls the 'new branded world' in which multi-national corporations have moved away from a focus on the marketing and sale of products, to the pro-motion of *brands* which endow their owners with 'corporate transcendence'. The Nike brand symbol is a ubiquitous swoosh, accompanied by the slogan 'Just Do It', which communicates a quasi-religious assurance of identity and well-being to consumers. In retail outlets called Nike Town, the swoosh, which is tattooed on the calves of many employees, is revered 'as both art and heroic symbol' (Klein: 2000, 56). Klein describes how a 24–year-old internet entrepreneur rationalises his decision to have the swoosh tattooed on his navel: 'I wake up every morning, jump in the shower, look down at the symbol, and that pumps me up for the day. It's just to remind me every day what I have to do, which is, "Just Do It".' (*ibid*.: 52) Clearly, the brand no longer signifies a mere product, but an entire philosophy and way of life.

What is occurring here is the commercialisation of both cultural and religious space and the colonising of the imaginative faculties of the young with the symbols of corporate organisations. This must be of great concern to Christians who struggle to discover faithful and relevant expressions of mission in the twenty-first century because underlying such developments at the deepest, world-view level, are claims that are simply false and idolatrous. As Jeremy Seabrook has said,

> Even the most privileged are compelled to bear within themselves the urgency for striving to acquire, the *compulsion* to wealth that has nothing to do with human need, but is part of a soulless system that we must inhabit and which inhabits and animates us. It is a form of *possession*, whereby we have come to identify our deepest human needs with the inescapable necessities of one particular economic system, so that we can no longer distinguish between our own unappeasable hunger and its insatiable search for profit.
>
> (Seabrook: 1988, 19 [emphasis mine])

Now, compare the perception and experience of the Nike brand symbol as described above with the way in which it is understood on the other side of the world, in the Asian factories in which the corporation's shoes are manufactured. Cikih Sukaesih is an Indonesian worker who was sacked by Nike for organising a strike to protest at working conditions. He reports that Asian labourers have always assumed that the slogan 'Just Do It' meant: 'Work harder and don't question authority' (Kundnani: 1999, 62). Here are the diverse human consequences of globalisation; it signals an apparent freedom for some (a freedom which may ultimately prove illusory), while on many others 'it descends as a cruel fate' (Bauman: 1998, 2).

The 'cruel fate' to which Zygmunt Bauman refers has both economic and social dimensions. With regard to the former, what is being global-ised is an economic philosophy and a system which allows and facilitates the transfer of wealth and power to a privileged minority unimpeded by political or social constraints. In the United States, older traditions of social democracy which defined freedom in relation to social and political ends, including the elimination of poverty, have been replaced by a new ideology in which democracy is simply *equated* with the function of unfettered free markets. The political and cultural triumph of this ideology has made possible an unprecedented upward transfer of wealth within America, a development which is now hailed as the triumph of *democracy*! At the global level, this same philosophy can justify a situation in which North American basketball and golfing stars are paid more in annual endorsement fees for branded products than the entire wage bill of the Asian workforce who actually manufac-ture these consumer goods. For the vast majority of the world's population, globalisation is experienced in terms of such grotesque inequalities as these, simply writ large. What is being globalised, says René Padilla, is a secular capitalist system which is 'almost totally ori-ented to the accumulation of wealth rather than to the satisfaction of basic human needs' (Padilla: 2001, 7).

Perhaps the chief social consequence of globalisation is related to the increased *mobility* that it makes possible for its beneficiaries. Whether by means of the unprecedented ability to move across geographical space as the result of the development of rapid, inter-continental trans-port systems, or through access to cyber space following the revolutionary growth of information technology, we are witnessing a movement of people and a diffusion of ideas across the planet on a scale that seems to mark a new era in human history. Once again, however, the impact of these changes is uneven and creates fresh and deep divisions within the human family. The mobility which is taken for granted by those whose economic resources give them access to virtually (no pun is intended) the whole world, is at the same time a powerfully *divisive* factor because for the majority of people on earth, those who are immobile and are tied by economic necessity to particular localities, 'the real space is fast closing up' (Bauman: 1998, 88).

Nothing illustrates this more dramatically than the spectacle of the two, totally contrasting forms of mobility which characterise our times. On the one hand, we witness the freely chosen travels of those who move around the globe as entrepreneurs or tourists, accumulating 'air miles' as they go and adding ever more exotic experiences to relate as travellers' tales back home. On the other hand, TV news bulletins present us with the dismal sight of a seemingly unstoppable flow of derelict humanity, *driven* to cross the continents in search of the means of survival. For the first group, living in 'the increasingly cosmopolitan, extraterritorial world of global businessmen, global cultural managers or global academics, state borders are levelled down, as they are dismantled for the world's commodities, capital and finances'. For the rest, the walls built of immigration controls and residence laws grow taller, and 'the moats separating them from the sites of their desire and of dreamed-of redemption grow deeper, while all bridges, at the first attempt to cross them, prove to be drawbridges' (*ibid.*: 89).

The implications of all this for the Christian mission are clearly enormous. On the one hand, it is increasingly evident that in the mysterious providence of God many of the most faithful and effective practitioners of mission in a globalised world are to be found among the poor and disenfranchised peoples who belong within the second group of travellers described above. This completely reverses the received expectations concerning the flow of mission within Christendom, undermining the assumption that Western Christianity possesses the spiritual, theological and material resources needed by the rest of the world. Like the church at Laodicea, which made very similar assumptions concerning itself, Christians in Europe and North America must recognise that their apparent wealth conceals an inner poverty and that the true riches are more likely to be found among non-Western believers for whom worship, faith and hope remain dynamic realities.

At the same time, the question raised in the previous chapter as to how Western Christians can articulate the Gospel with credibility among the poor of the earth when they themselves are inevitably found alongside global business people and academics among the privileged elite of the world, comes into yet clearer focus. The Peruvian theologian Samuel Escobar has pointed out that the culture of globalisation creates a mental frame among those who benefit from it that may be diametrically opposed to 'what the gospel teaches about human life under God's design'. Escobar warns that if mission simply 'rides on the crest of the globalization wave' it runs the risk of subverting the core meaning of the Gospel (Escobar: 2000, 30–31). Perhaps, then, the primary missiological task for the Western churches will be found in relation to the profound existential needs of the global travellers in the first group described above. The phenomena of global tourism, or the search for second, or third, dream homes in paradise locations, or even the escape into the cyber-world – all of these may be symptoms of a profound cultural malaise in Western societies, derived from a sense of homelessness which is, in the final analysis, metaphysical in character. As the following chapter will make clear, the challenge posed by this particular culture may represent the highest priority in mission for the churches in the Western world today, while presenting them with the greatest and most dangerous task they have ever confronted.

Globalisation and Localisation

In the summer of 1993, Samuel Huntington published an article with the title 'The Clash of Civilizations?' which provoked widespread, and continuing, debate. Huntington's thesis, which he later elaborated in *The Clash of Civilizations and the Remaking of World Order*, was that talk of the 'triumph of the West' was profoundly misleading since it ignored the reawakening and resurgence of a variety of ancient civilisational identities and values around the world. Dazzled by the technological brilliance of the West, many cultural analysts had failed to recognise that the long period of Western expansion and dominance had triggered a variety of cultural and religious reactions which meant that 'the unidirectional impact of one civilization on all others' was being replaced by a new era of 'intense, sustained, and multidirectional interactions among all civilizations' (Huntington: 1998, 53). Huntington describes what he calls the 'Davos Culture' shared by a thousand businessmen, bankers, intellectuals and politicians who meet annually at the World Economic Forum in Switzerland. This group controls practically all existing global institutions and its members have their hands on the most important levers of economic and military power in the world. And yet, despite its undoubted importance and global reach, this culture is shared by a small minority of the world's population while, outside this privileged coterie, the world seethes with forces of resistance, reaction and opposition, often inspired by resurgent religions. Within these reviving civilisations, people are able to make a critical and selective appropriation of *modernity* while challenging the secular values and philosophy of the Western world. Thus, the Chinese seek to modernise while returning to Confucian values, Russia adopts a similar strategy involving a fusion of modernity with a revitalised Orthodoxy, and the worldwide Islamic resurgence combines a selective use of modern science and technology with an emphatic repudiation of Western culture and a renewed commitment to a radically theistic world-view. In a sentence which, in the aftermath of the destruction of the World Trade Center in New York in September 2001, sounds like a chilling prophecy, Huntington wrote: 'Somewhere in the Middle East a half-dozen young men could well be dressed in jeans, drinking Coke, listening to rap, and, between their bows to Mecca, *putting together a bomb to blow up an American airliner*' (*ibid.*: 58 [emphasis mine]).

The realisation that the processes of globalisation are paralleled by, and result in, movements of local resistance, reaction and protest, has led sociologists to employ the term *glocalisation* in order to describe the complex inter-relation between these two phenomena. In this way recognition is given to the realities of both the increasing uniformity of institutions and behaviour around the world *and* the appearance and growth of rediscovered local identities, cultures and religions. In fact, according to Zygmunt Bauman, the two things are intimately related to each other, so that the growing polarisation among the peoples of the world is not an external interference with the process of globalisation but *is its effect* (Bauman: 1998, 93).

A case study from India may help to illustrate the manner in which these two seemingly contradictory movements function together in a symbiotic, cause-and-effect manner. Arundhati Roy describes the growth of 'call centres' in Asia, in which thousands of educated young people are trained to provide the customer service operations of trans-national corporations. Colleges have been established in cities like Delhi and Bangalore in which potential employees are trained in the use of American and British accents in order that callers from those countries enquiring about a credit card balance, or a malfunctioning washing machine, will be unaware of the location of their advisor. Indian students are required to read foreign newspapers or, when acting as medical secretaries for American hospitals, to watch TV medical dramas like ER which familiarise them with the terminology and culture of hospitals in the United States. When on duty, Indian names are replaced by Anglicised versions: Sushma becomes Susie, Govind is replaced by Jerry, and Advani answers to Andy. In other words, educated Indians are being de-cultured in order to make them employable, at one-tenth of the salaries of their counter-parts in the West, in the globalised economy.

By contrast, India is witnessing a resurgence of militant nationalist Hinduism as an expression of a 'terrible backlash against this enforced abasement'. Within this movement, according to Roy, ordinary people learn that 'amassing nuclear weapons, religious bigotry, misogyny, homophobia, book burning and outright hatred are the ways to retrieve a nation's lost dignity'. What is even more disturbing, however, is that these two contrasting scenarios reveal the operation of the symbiosis between the globalised economy and local ethnic and religious re-actions since, while one arm of the Indian government 'is busy selling the nation off in chunks', another arm is 'orchestrating a baying, howling, deranged chorus of cultural nationalism'. Arundhati Roy con-cludes that what is happening today is 'almost too colossal for human comprehension' and that, in this context, 'the only thing in the world worth globalising, is dissent' (Roy: 2001, 14–15).

Globalisation from Below

I referred earlier to the *positive* aspects of globalisation and it is time to return to a consideration of these. Although the last sentence quoted from Roy above might be read as a despairing, even cynical, expression of the hopelessness arising from the negative experience of the global-ising process, it can (and I think, should) be understood as pointing toward the manner in which the new context in which we find ourselves makes possible dissent, resistance and a global debate concerning alter-native visions of the future of humankind. Indeed, this is illustrated by the fact that Arundhati Roy's article, entitled 'The Reincarnation of Rumpelstiltskin', was available to me on the other side of the globe by means of the worldwide web. This aspect of globalisation has been described by Ulrich Beck in words that have obvious relevance to our concerns with the future of the Christian mission:

> Globality means that from now on nothing which happens on our planet is only a limited local event; all inventions, victories and catas-trophes affect the whole world, and we must reorient and reorganize our lives and actions, our organizations and institutions, along a 'local-global' axis. (Beck: 2000, 11)

Beck mounts a detailed critique of what he calls 'globalism', by which he means the spread of the economistic culture we have described, in which 'a social revolution from above' passes itself off as non-political. *Globalism* views the future through the single lens of the market economy and, bypassing political, ethical and religious values, involves 'a form of *one-dimensional* thinking and acting, a *mono-causal* econo-mistic view of the world' (*ibid.*: 118). And yet, while this ideological globalism must be exposed for what it is and vigorously resisted, what

Beck calls *globality* opens up an unprecedented opportunity for dialogue, reflection and the articulation of new visions for the future of the human family. Thus, for example, globalisation has resulted in the discovery that the act of purchase, or non-purchase, *'can always and everywhere be a direct ballot-paper*. The boycott can thus join and combine active consumer society with direct democracy – on a world scale' (*ibid.*: 70). What this means is that the present situation need not be viewed in entirely negative or apocalyptic terms, since it creates new space and opportunity for the growth of truly counter-cultural communities shaped by alternative hopes and visions for the future of humankind.

The distinction being made here can be expressed in different terms by the use of the categories of 'globalisation from *above* and from *below*'. The former refers to the spread of economism and is a reconstruction of the processes of imperialism in which the institutions of Western capitalism 'send out voracious tentacles all over the globe seeking markets and profits' to the advantage of an already rich and powerful minority based mainly in North America and Europe. But there is a globalisation of a different kind, resulting from person-to-person contacts through the activities of Non-Governmental Organisations, cultural exchange programmes and the work of missions. The so-called 'short-term' programmes of missionary organisations have exposed thousands of young Christians from the West to the cultural, religious, social and economic realities of peoples in the southern hemisphere and for very many this experience, however brief, has been life-transforming. This is globalisation *from below*, driven not by the search for profit but by a spirit of human solidarity and compassion. Such experiences, together with the explosion of information made possible by the new technologies, is resulting in a situation in which both human tragedies and their causes become vividly real to millions of people among the privileged of the earth, so stimulating a movement which results in the universalising of compassion. As the Australian theologian Allan Patience puts it, the potential exists today for a fruitful dialogue across ethnic and religious boundaries which could be 'a loving counter to the threats of a clash of civilizations'. Consequently, Christians should be less in awe of globalisation from above and more excited by 'the human possibilities in globalisation from below' (Patience: 1999, 243–4).

Following Jesus in a Globalised World

We began this chapter with the art of Hieronymus Bosch and I suggested that the fantastic imagery found on his canvasses seems to anticipate the moral chaos and nihilism with which we have now become familiar. You will recall John Berger's suggestion that in a world gone mad the only hope for the future lies in establishing 'pockets of resistance' in which Bosch's paintings can be studied 'by torchlight in the dark'. This proposal dovetails with the concept of globalisation from below, which has been discussed above. However, I want to suggest that specifically as a Christian artist, Bosch has more to say to us than this and that in his overtly religious paintings we may discover important clues concerning the practice of mission in our times.

Let us reflect, first, on the *image of Christ* in this artist's work. Having examined the fantastic and lurid imagery to be found in his greatest masterpieces, expressing visions that take us beyond mundane reality to the realms of the supernatural, the demonic, and perhaps the subconcious, we might anticipate that Bosch's treatment of the story of the passion of Jesus would focus attention on these aspects. And indeed, some pictures, like a painting now in Ghent entitled *Christ Carrying the Cross*, do connect with these themes by representing the hostility of Christ's enemies in a manner that clearly suggests the underlying presence and activity of demonic powers. Walter Gibson describes the malice reflected on the contorted and ugly faces that surround Jesus as reaching 'hysterical pitch' and Bosch clearly intends us to conclude that these people are on the verge of forfeiting their claim to be human beings. Here then is the familiar Bosch, the painter of the fantastic and subliminal who digs beneath the surface level of things to expose the depths of the subconscious and the spiritual.

However, when we stand before a painting in the National Gallery in London entitled *Christ Mocked (The Crowning with Thorns)* (picture 9) it is as though we have entered another world. Gone are the fantastic images and symbols for which Bosch is chiefly remembered today, and even the hints of demonic activity in the Ghent picture are entirely absent here. Instead, the beautiful face of Jesus – calm, focused, imploring – is surrounded by enemies who are 'all too human'. These are real people, representing different classes in medieval society, yet united in their uncontrollable anger, intense envy and unremitting hatred toward the gentle Christ. From the central point of the picture, Jesus looks directly at us, suggesting that there is an alternative way to the mainstream path of carnality and greed, and inviting us to follow him.

This brings us to the second great lesson we can learn from Bosch's art, which concerns the *life of discipleship*. Hieronymus Bosch must have read and pondered a book which was a key text in a movement of religious renewal in Holland during his lifetime, Thomas à Kempis' *The Imitation of Christ*. What he learned from this author was that true Christianity was both radical in its moral and ethical demands and counter-cultural in relation to a world in thrall to idols: 'Whoever desires to understand and take delight in the words of Christ,' said à Kempis, '*must strive to conform his whole life to Him*' (à Kempis: 1952, 27). Bosch's art makes this choice crystal clear, offering us a way out of the madness of the world that is neither a form of escapism nor a soft option, but a following of Christ which will inevitably involve us, as it did him, in rejection and suffering.

Thus, while Christians will gladly join those who want to study *The Garden of Earthly Delights* in the dark by torchlight, they will also want to turn the beam towards the hauntingly beautiful image of Jesus in *Christ Crowned With Thorns*, in the belief that the one depicted there can guide them in living and witnessing faithfully at the new frontier of mission in a globalised world. Bosch's painting provides a brilliant visual commentary on words with which he was doubtless familiar:

> When Jesus is with us, all is well, and nothing seems hard; but when Jesus is absent, everything is difficult. When Jesus does not speak to the heart, all other comfort is unavailing; but if Jesus speaks but a single word, we are greatly comforted. (à Kempis: 1952, 76)

7

A Biblical Model:
Confessing Jesus as Lord in Eternal Rome

The book of Revelation, with its apocalyptic visions and subtle, complex symbolism has perplexed generations of readers and preachers. It has also been rather marginal in discussions of the biblical theology of mission. Both Roman Catholic studies (Senior and Stuhlmueller: 1983, 302–305) and those from a Protestant perspective (Köstenberger and O'Brien: 2001, 243–9) have treated Revelation in the space of few pages, giving the impression that it contains little of significance with regard to the understanding of the Christian mission in the New Testament. Indeed, according to Köstenberger and O'Brien, Revelation presents the reader 'with a powerful vision of the results of the Christian mission at the end of time' and urges believers to 'fix their hope on the eternal world awaiting them', a world that is said to be 'even more real and permanent than the realities of this present life, which are merely temporary and transitional' (*ibid.*: 243–4).

The problem with this kind of approach is that it obscures the vital fact that the theology of Revelation is, to use a term familiar within mission studies, highly *contextual*. The author is not presenting us with an ahistorical mysticism unrelated to time and place, nor does he offer a 'spiritual' view of reality which removes us from concerns about politics and economics. John's first readers lived their daily lives in the cities of the Roman empire where, at every turn, they were confronted by reminders of the power and success of this system. Even now, two thousand years later, one cannot fail to be impressed by the glory that was Rome, whether glimpsing it in the ruins of the ancient city which was at the centre of this extraordinary empire, or trekking beside Hadrian's Wall as it snakes its way across the hills of northern England at the periphery of Roman power. To enter the Pantheon in Rome, notwithstanding its conversion into a church, is to feel an unnerving sense of the attractive power of the ideology of the Roman empire and of its undoubted cultural and economic achievements. Here was an empire that, in its military and economic dominance over the then-known world, was both *global* in its reach and *economistic* in its essential character. Consider, for example, this revealing statement by the Roman orator Aelius Aristides, delivered before the imperial court in Rome in about AD 155:

> Here is brought from every land and sea all the crops of the seasons and the produce of each land, river, lake, as well as the arts of the Greeks and barbarians, so that if someone should wish to view all these things, he must either see them by travelling over the whole world or be in this city . . . It is possible to see so many cargoes from India and even from Arabia . . . that one imagines that for the future the trees are left bare for the people there and that they must come here to beg for their own produce if they need anything . . . Whatever one does not see here, is not a thing which has existed or exists, so that it is not easy to decide which has the greater superiority, the city in regard to present day cities, or the empire in regard to the empires that have gone before.
>
> (Quoted in Bauckham: 1993a, 375)

Clearly Aristides, as a beneficiary of the empire, exults in its achievements and presents these in line with the official ideology, as irrefutable evidence of the success of Rome and of its destiny to bring human history to its culmination and completion. It was in precisely this context that the early church came to birth and, in particular, the final book in the Bible came to be written.

The Biblical Critique of Rome

The churches we encounter in the book of Revelation are, for the most part, weak and demoralised. With few exceptions, they were either cowed by Roman power or seduced by its success. Indeed, some of them are in such an advanced state of syncretism that they stand on the very brink of total apostasy. Aristides came from the city of Smyrna where, Revelation informs us, Christians faced 'afflictions . . . poverty . . . slander' and suffering (Rev. 2:9). In this dire situation, says Richard Bauckham, John and his readers are 'taken up into heaven in order to see the world from the heavenly perspective'. This is not, as Karl Marx

105

would have it, a false consciousness which serves only to buttress the power of the privileged and the oppressor. On the contrary:

> The effect of John's visions . . . is to expand his readers' world . . . to open their world to divine transcendence. The bounds which Roman power and ideology set to the readers' world are broken open and that world is seen as open to the greater purpose of its transcendent Creator and Lord. (Bauckham: 1993b, 7)

This movement from the world of time and space in which Roman power appears to be the only ultimate reality, into another dimension of knowledge and experience, occurs immediately after the dismal descriptions of the churches which has filled chapters 2 and 3: '*After this I looked*, and there before me was a door standing open in heaven. And the voice . . . said, "Come up here, and I will show you what must take place after this" ' (4:1). The simple fact to be observed here is that the open door which the writer glimpses in this vision signals the existence of an *exit* from the present reality. There is a way out of the madness of the known world and the prospect of an *alternative* view of human life and purpose to that promoted in Rome. In a Bosch-like world without horizons, where all hope of change has been eliminated by a propoganda machine that insists that the ultimate destiny of the human race has been revealed by Rome, suddenly a new horizon becomes visible and human hope revives.

However, once John, and his readers with him, pass through this door, *everything is changed*. This is most emphatically not an escape to a never-never land in which the adherents of an other-worldly form of religion dispense large doses of opium to those who might be inclined to question the dominant view of reality. On the contrary, the vision of the throne of the creator God, which immediately comes into view on the other side of the door, makes possible the unmasking of the absurd and blasphemous pretensions of Rome and results in the discovery that the empire is, in truth, 'a system of violent oppression, founded on conquest, maintained by violence and oppression' (Bauckham: 1993b, 35).

In fact, once this extraordinary work is understood and read within its context, the radical nature of its critique of Roman power and ideology can be seen as simply breathtaking in its clarity and boldness. It operates not at the level of rational argument, but rather in relation to the human *imagination*, employing symbols and visual imagery so as to purge the Christian consciousness and then renew it with an alternative perception of the world and its destiny. Thus, the victorious and apparently glorious Roman army, which through its conquests had laid the foundations for the empire, becomes in John's vision *a hideous beast* which has terrified the inhabitants of the earth and seems to them to be invincible (13:1–4). The city of Rome itself, boasting of its superiority to every other urban development in human history, is represented in Revelation as *a prostitute* (17:1–5). Indeed, the picture we are given here is not that of an ordinary harlot, but of a rich court-esan, able to maintain a luxurious lifestyle at the expense of her clients throughout the empire. Roman ideology made much of the supposed benefits which the *Pax Romana* bestowed on subject peoples, yet in John's view even these advantages were illusory since they were purchased at the high price of economic exploitation.

The critique of Rome, and the announcement of divine judgement upon it for its blasphemies and wickedness, reaches its climax in the spine-chilling description of the fall of Babylon in chapter 18. John identifies three classes of people throughout the empire who, having profited from the Roman system, are now stupified and aghast at the prospect of its collapse and destruction: the '*kings* of the earth' (18:9), the '*merchants*' (18:11) and the *mariners*, who between them made possible the transfer of the wealth of the world to the city of Rome (18:17). This chapter contains a quite extraordinary list of the cargoes which were brought from the extreme limits of the known world, including gold, silver, silk, ivory, marble and spices of many kinds. The trade in these commodities was already leading to the exhaustion of the earth and the destruction of species, with the market in ivory placing the Syrian elephant under threat of extinction. Concern for God's creation and the recognition of the ecological impact of this economistic culture is doubtless reflected in the announcement of judgement on those 'who destroy the earth' (11:18). Just how far-flung were Roman trading links becomes clear when the origins of the items listed above are identified, since such study reveals that the trade network extended as far afield as Yemen, Africa, India, Ceylon, Indonesia and China (18:11–13). Clearly, Aristides did not exaggerate when he said that the produce from 'every land and sea' found its way to the city of Rome.

At the conclusion of this list of commodities the reader is suddenly jolted by the phrase, '*and the bodies and souls of men*' (18:13). This detail reminds us, should we need such confirmation, that the issues here are not merely 'economic', but moral and ethical because the prosperity of Rome was built on the practice of *slavery.* John's statement thus serves not only to expose and condemn such practice, but it also affirms the human dignity and worth of the untold thousands of people who have been so humiliated and mistreated. Clearly, the visionary nature of this book is not a way of escaping from concrete political and economic realities, but is rather a means by which the power of Rome is subjected to a searching prophetic critique.

The Victory of Christ

A key moment in John's narrative is found at the point at which, having been shown a scroll sealed with seven seals in the right hand of God, he learns that no one 'in heaven or on earth or under the earth could open the scroll or even look inside it' (5:3). John confesses that he wept bitterly and uncontrollably that the search for a person *worthy* to open the scroll appears to have ended in failure. Here is a moment of great dramatic tension which suggests that the content of this scroll is crucial to the message of Revelation as a whole and that failure to gain access to the information it contains will mean the ultimate triumph of Rome. If the seals cannot be broken then we appear to be shut up in a world without a transcendent purpose, where the will to power is endless and human hope becomes mere wishful thinking.

At this vital moment John is told to dry his eyes and his attention is directed to 'the Lion of the Tribe of Judah' who *is able* to break the seven seals. John looks and sees 'a Lamb, looking as if it had been slain' (5:5–6). This is the same person before whom he has already fallen prostrate at the start of the book, the Christ who declares, 'I am the First and the Last. I am the Living One; I was dead, and behold I am alive for ever and ever! And I hold the keys of death and Hades' (1:17–18). Suddenly, heaven rings with a new song in honour of the one who is '*worthy* to take the scroll and to open its seals' (5:9). From this point on the contents of the scroll are unfolded through many chapters and it becomes clear that the central theme of the book concerns the *transfer* of sovereignty over the world from the beast and the harlot to God and his Christ.

In the previous chapter we suggested that it is possible to identify two forms of globalisation, one from *above,* imposed by arbitrary power and resulting in multiple divisions within the human family, and the other from *below,* a revolution of love and compassion which respects and values the differences between peoples while affirming their fundamental unity and human dignity. Similar contrasting forms of universalism are to be found in the book of Revelation. On the one hand, John repeatedly employs phrases such as 'the inhabitants of the earth' (19:2) in a negative sense to describe the nations and peoples in their subjection to the false and corrupting power of the Roman empire. The 'inhabitants of the earth' have been seduced by promises of prosperity and well-being and have become drunk with the wine of Rome's adulteries (17:2). Here is a false approach to globalisation, built on wrong foundations, compromised by terrible forms of idolatry, and resulting in untold human misery and division.

On the other hand, John catches sight of and develops the biblical vision of a universalism built on entirely different foundations which will result in a numberless multitude 'from every nation, tribe, people and language' standing 'before the throne and in front of the Lamb' (7:9). It is important to observe that Revelation here anticipates a process of change, a transformation in which the peoples of the world withdraw their allegiance from the beast and the harlot and enter the kingdom of God. We are bound to ask here a question which has deep missiological significance: *how does this change come about?*

The Issue of Discipleship

The letters addressed to the seven churches in chapters 2 and 3 all end with the same exhortation to 'hear what the Spirit says to the churches' (2:7, 11, 17, 29; 3:6, 13, 22). This suggests that the activity of the Holy Spirit is dynamic and contemporary; the demand is to listen to the voice of God *now*, in the present situation. The witness of the Spirit at Pentecost and the revelation then granted to the churches as they came to birth and grew in strength is not denied or withdrawn, but now a later generation, facing new challenges to faith and obedience, needs to hear the Spirit afresh.

What is more, there is an *ecumenical* dimension to this statement. Each of these letters is clearly related, as many studies have shown, to the specific context in which the particular congregations find themselves. Their local challenges are known and understood, together with the specific triumphs and failures that are characteristic of the individual churches. Thus, they must obviously listen carefully to the letter addressed to them and respond to the particular words of pastoral and prophetic instruction which it contains. And yet, the instruction remains to hear 'what the Spirit says to the *churches*'. In other words, it is through active fellowship with each other and the recognition that each group has something to learn from the rest, that the total message communicated by the Spirit can be heard and obeyed. We are reminded here of the legitimate theological pluralism discussed in an earlier chapter, and it is clear that no single church has a monopoly on the Spirit or the word. Different traditions, and churches from many cultural contexts, have something vital to contribute to the total picture and only through such genuinely ecumenical fellowship will it be possible for Christians to discern the mind of Christ. Indeed, Justo Gonzalez suggests that the emergence of a genuinely multicultural church and the theological and spiritual implications of this is one of the key themes of Revelation and, relating this to our situation, he comments:

> The fact is that the gospel *is* making headway among the many tribes, nations, and languages – that it is indeed making more headway among them than it is among the dominant cultures of the North Atlantic. The question is not whether there will be a multicultural church. Rather, the question is whether those who have become so accustomed to seeing the gospel expressed only or primarily in terms of those dominant cultures will be able to participate in the life of the multicultural church that is already a reality (Gonzalez: 1999, 91)

In addition, one other phrase is common to each of these letters; it is the summons to '*overcome*'. Again, what is to be overcome in each situation is related to the specific threats to faith and holiness identified in each of the letters, but the *common* danger confronting all the churches without exception is that constituted by the global culture of Rome. Indeed, the theme of 'overcoming', of conquering in the face of terrible evil, is a central strand in the book as a whole and, as we shall see shortly, it points us towards the answer to our question as to how the missionary witness of the church can be successful.

The description of the fall of Babylon in chapter 18 is accompanied by an exhortation to Christian believers: 'Come out of her, my people, so that you will not share in her sins' (18:4). The significance of this call lies in the fact that it assumes that many Christians in this period were themselves deeply immersed in the trade and commerce of the empire and were beneficiaries of the system. More than that, since they had personally prospered by operating within the system, they were inclined to believe the Roman propaganda and so to seek a synthesis between Christ and Caesar. The seven letters discussed above were addressed to churches located in prosperous cities which, as ports or commercial and administrative centres, were deeply embedded within Roman economic, cultural and religious structures. Thus, while some of the first readers of this book were undoubtedly poor and suffering, others were affluent, comfortable and deeply compromised. We have noted several times the obvious case of the church at Laodicea, which boasted of its wealth and material success. Elsewhere we discover a prophetess operating within the church at Thyatira who promotes a form of religion which undermines the agreement reached at the Council of Jerusalem, as reported in Acts 15, and seeks to replace the Christian ethic with sexual norms operative within the pagan, Roman world (2:18). Facts like these enable us to understand why Revelation devotes so much space to the anguish of the beneficiaries of the Roman system at the sight of its collapse and total destruction. The truth is that the ruling classes, the commercial magnates and those with a stake in the transportation of goods across the world obviously included many professing Christians who were able to say, 'I am rich; I have acquired wealth and do not need a thing' (3:17). Thus, John's critique of the empire 'did more than voice the protest of groups exploited, oppressed and persecuted by Rome. It also required those who would share in her profits to side with her victims and become victims themselves' (Bauckham: 1993a, 378).

At this point we need to return to the content of the scroll sealed with seven seals which, as we noted earlier, is central to the message of the book of Revelation. At the heart of the visions which follow the opening of the scroll by the Lamb 'looking as if it had been slain', we encounter two witnesses whose story, so John is told, concerns 'many peoples, nations, languages and kings' (10:11). That is to say, the message contained in this vision is *universal* in its reach and concerns the salvation of all the peoples on earth. Within this text, therefore, we may anticipate the discovery of an answer to the question posed earlier as to precisely how the missionary witness of the church will result in the nations transferring their loyalty and worship from the idols that presently hold them in thrall to the one who alone is worthy 'to receive glory and honour and power' (4:11).

As the vision unfolds we learn that the faithful and uncompromising witness of the two prophets provokes the wrath of the beast from the Abyss who attacks and kills them, leaving their bodies lying in the street of the great city 'where also their Lord was crucified' (11:8). In this and other respects, the witnesses follow the pattern set by the life, death and resurrection of their Lord. Initially, the 'inhabitants of the earth'

111

gloat over the corpses of the witnesses, sending gifts to each other to celebrate the death of those whose testimony had 'tormented' them. But now comes a crucial turning point in the narrative when, after life is restored to the martyrs and they are taken up into heaven, the peoples at last turn away from the beast and give glory 'to the God of heaven'. Loud voices are now heard from heaven announcing that 'The kingdom of the world has become the kingdom of our Lord and his Christ' (11:15).

What makes this passage so important in relation to our concerns with Christian mission in a globalised world is that it reveals the divine strategy whereby the nations are brought to repentance and the worship of God. What divine judgements alone have failed to accomplish, *a suffering church, following its Lord in faithful witness unto death, does achieve*. The missiology of the book of Revelation thus has little to do with efficiency of method or the use of superior techniques; its focus is rather upon the need for witnesses to be ready to endure 'great tribulation' (7:14) and not to love their lives so much 'as to shrink from death' (12:11). This theme of prophetic witness, modelled on the example of Jesus, is discovered to be at the very heart of the book when we recognise that the two witnesses in chapter 11 *represent the whole church in its missionary witness throughout the final period of human history.* This text, so understood, makes it clear that the liberation and healing of the nations, the reaping of the harvest made possible through the sacrifice of Christ, comes about only through the witness of a church willing to endure rejection and martyrdom.

The Apocalypse and Globalisation

There are obviously many parallels between the situation facing the churches described in Revelation and the context within which we seek to discover a faithful pattern of mission today. Clearly, caution is needed in making the move from this biblical text to the contemporary frontier of mission provided by globalisation. We must not ignore the fact that centuries of history have intervened between then and now, including the evangelisation of the very empire against which John directed his prophetic critique. Nonetheless, as we have seen earlier, biblical prophecy continues to speak with power and relevance long after the age in which it was originally given and the book of Revelation is certainly no exception in this regard. In the same way that John recognised the Roman empire as the successor of both Babylon and Tyre and concluded that it must fall under the same judgement of God which earlier prophets had announced to those kingdoms, so his own prophecy transcends its original reference and applies wherever similar forms of idolatry and wickedness become pervasive and powerful. In this way, the Apocalypse 'has inspired prophetic critiques of later systems of political and economic oppression throughout the church's history and still does so today' (Bauckham: 1993b, 153).

In the first half of the twentieth century, facing the rise of Nazism and the tendency of the German churches to seek a new accommodation with this particular Caesar, Dietrich Bonhoeffer insisted that a faithful, truly confessing church, 'must be a community which hears the Apocalypse'. At the very same time, months before the Nazis annexed Austria, the composer Franz Schmidt wrote an oratorio with the title *Das Buch mit Sieben Siegeln* ('The Book with Seven Seals'). Based on the words of Luther's translation of the Apocalypse, this work, although largely unknown in the English-speaking world, is regarded as a masterpiece in central Europe. As the beast and the harlot once again stalked the earth, Schmidt set the words of the book of Revelation to music of such power and beauty that those who heard the first performance in Vienna in 1938 could not fail to 'hear the Apocalypse' and understand its prophetic significance afresh. As an invading army, representing a racist creed and an idolatrous state, stood poised to invade Austria, Schmidt reminded people of a different way of seeing the world as his soloist sang the Lamb who had been slain, and the chorus responded with the words: 'He hath redeemed us with his blood, from *every* kindred and tongue and people and nation'. It seems that the Nazis realised only too well the significance of this work and after the *Anschluss* the composer was treated with contempt, became seriously ill and died in 1939.

What might it mean for us today, in the era of globalisation, to *hear the Apocalypse*? And what relevance does all of this have to the emerging paradigm of Christian mission? I suggest that among the many lessons this book has to teach us, there are three that are of particular significance. First, Revelation reminds us of the central importance of *worship* in the life of the missionary church. In the New Testament there is simply no distinction between worship and mission, the one flows out of the other and indeed, returns to its source, since the objective of the witness of the church in the world is that all peoples should be brought to share in the privilege and joy of worshipping the living God. In fact, worship does far more than simply energise mission, it is itself a fundamental aspect of the very being of the missionary church. In the Apocalypse, to go through the door that stands open in heaven and so to enter the throne room of the transcendent God is more than simply a spiritual act (although it is that), it is a subversive move which inevitably calls into question the claims of the dominant ideology. Thus, to enter the church and identify with a community that 'hears the Apocalypse' and worships God, is to place oneself in danger. Clearly, this raises vital questions concerning contemporary worship and requires a radical rethinking of many received traditions concerning the practice of mission.

Secondly, the prominence given to the human *imagination* in this book points us towards a vital principle with regard to Christian communication in a world dominated by symbols and visual imagery. In an economistic culture in which, as we have seen, business corporations spend vast amounts of money promoting brand images and seeking to colonise the imaginative lives of young people, it is vital that we recognise the missiological significance of the fact that the Apocalypse was designed to bring about a purging and renewing of the Christian imagination. Too often mission has bypassed people's imaginative faculties, addressing them at a rational and intellectual level and running the risk of producing converts suffering from a kind of spiritual schizophrenia. The Apocalypse reminds us that cultures are formed not merely by ideas, important as they undoubtedly are, but also by visions, images and ideals, and the Christian mission dare not overlook the importance of this dimension.

Finally, perhaps the most important lesson the book of Revelation has for Christians in the modern Western world concerns the nature of discipleship and the cost of following Jesus in the age of globalisation. Addressing an audience of Western missionary leaders and practitioners, the Sri Lankan theologian Ajith Fernando observed that Christians from the churches in the West appeared to be finding it increasingly difficult to cope with the demands of life outside a culture which offers them wealth, pleasure and comfort. Missionaries from the affluent parts of the world, said Fernando, 'may be losing their ability to live with inconvenience, stress and hardship, as there is more and more emphasis on comfort and convenience'. In the age of globalisation it might be that the West will 'soon disqualify itself from being a missionary-sending region' (Fernando: 1999, 25).

We surely hear in these words the echo of the voice that spoke to the churches in danger of capitulation to the materialism of Rome in the first century: *'He who has an ear, let him hear what the Spirit says to the churches'.*

8

Mission at the New Frontiers

In the first chapter of this book I indicated the intention to search for the new frontiers of mission today and, in the light of the discovery of these, to consider the mental, structural and theological changes that will be needed if the church is to obey Christ in relevant and faithful witness in this new context. Having now completed our exploration of the postmodern frontiers of mission, we must conclude with an attempt to provide critical reflection on the practice of mission in this situation and offer some indication of the possible ways forward.

What is clear by now is that both the *concept* of mission as a one-way movement from Christendom to the unevangelised world, and the *structures* devised at the close of the eighteenth century to facilitate that movement, have been overtaken by historical developments that render them increasingly irrelevant and redundant. At this point the distinction between *mission*, as the abiding obligation and mark of the church of Christ at all times and in all places, and *missions*, signifying specific, historically conditioned institutions created to advance the cause of the kingdom of God in particular cultural situations, becomes vitally important. To fail to make this distinction, and therefore to identify a specific inherited paradigm of mission and its organisational structures with mission itself, is to risk being locked into an obsolete model and so to be condemned to increasingly futile and frustrating activity. Any serious study of the history of the Christian mission leads to the conclusion that, while the cross-cultural transmission of the faith constitutes the very lifeblood of the church and is one of its most vital religious characteristics, the means and methods by which this has been done are various and many. Thus, while *mission* is a biblical universal, the *modern missionary movement* was a specific, culturally conditioned initiative which, while amazingly successful in its time, is likely to become increasingly dysfunctional if the attempt is made to preserve it in the new context we have described. From this perspective it is possible to accept without anxiety or regret the verdict of historians that the modern missionary movement has almost reached the end of its life:

> The missionary movement is now in its old age. It is not a useless and decrepit old age. There are situations where it provides the most effective, perhaps the only foreseeable means of making any witness to Christ or any proclamation about him . . . But the conditions that produced the movement have changed, and they have been changed by the Lord of history. And the church has been changed out of all recognition by the agency of the missionary movement itself.
>
> (Walls: 1996, 261)

Mission after Christendom

In the first chapter of this book we noticed the way in which certain habits of thought derived from the so-called 'great ages of faith' linger on, shaping people's perceptions of the missionary task long after the structures in which these ideas came to birth have decayed and been abandoned. The missionary hymns of the second half of the nineteenth and early twentieth centuries, for example, breathe a spirit of confidence in the success of the enterprise and anticipate that the global spread of the Gospel will result in the rapid displacement of other faiths. Under the influence of modern Western culture, which was confident, expansionist and profoundly shaped by evolutionary assumptions, the church came to assume that it was destined to expand across the world, replacing ancient religions and plotting its onward and upward growth with only minor and temporary setbacks and reversals. Robert Speer, writing just before the outbreak of the First World War in *The Fundamentals* (the volumes that gave their name to the movement that became known as 'Fundamentalism'), said that 'the intention to conquer' was characteristic of Christianity. In its missionary advance around the globe, Speer said, the attitude of the church is 'not one of compromise, but one of conflict and conquest. It proposes to displace the other religions' (Speer: n.d., 84). Such a notion of missionary advance, in which the ancient religions of Africa and Asia are to be replaced by Christianity in the form known to the missionaries, easily led to distorted views in which the church, equipped with the wealth and technology believed to be the fruit of its superior civilisation, became confident of its ability to manage continuous, quantifiable and measurable progress. In this process the Holy Spirit became functionally redundant.

Of course, it remains true that, whatever the shape of the emerging, postmodern paradigm of mission, Christians are bound to continue to hope and pray that God's kingdom *will come* and that his will may be done *on earth, as in heaven*. The horizon of hope in the Bible extends to the ends of the earth and the farthest limits of the cosmos and, as we have seen, the book of Revelation anticipates a time when the nations will transfer their allegiance from the Caesars who lead them astray, to the living God. Christianity is indeed a global movement and the purpose of missionary witness is inextricably linked to the biblical vision of a new and redeemed humankind, united in the glad worship of its Creator and Saviour. However, the very fact that, in obedience to Christ, we continually *pray* for this outcome is a reminder that the growth of the kingdom is a divine gift and that, while we are called to bear witness to the reality of God's reign through Christ, the Lord himself continues to work in the world, building that kingdom in ways that defy human perception and analysis. We need to be reminded that the historical path which leads to the desired and prayed-for end sometimes passes through dark and gloomy valleys and trackless wastelands. A biblical theology of mission, as well as the study of the history of mission, leads to the conclusion that the wilderness belongs to God as much as does the well-watered garden and there are times when his purpose requires that the church goes through the former rather than dwells in the latter. God only knows when the compromise of the church reaches such a level that it requires purging through judgement, but the promise of the presence of the Spirit is given to faithful disciples whatever the terrain through which they pass, whether in the desert or in the promised land, whether facing the great tribulation or standing on the edge of the glory of the millennium. What is needed is faith in the *final* triumph of God and a reverent agnosticism as to *how*, in a fallen and confused world, that desired goal will be reached. Such faith is beautifully expressed in the lines of the Victorian hymn writer, William Fullerton:

> *I cannot tell how* he will win the nations,
> *How* he will claim his earthly heritage,

How satisfy the needs and aspirations
Of east and west, of sinner and of sage.
But this I know, all flesh shall see his glory,
And he shall reap the harvest he has sown,
And some glad day his sun will shine in splendour,
When he the Saviour, Saviour of the world is known.

The fact is that the history of mission is replete with examples of the way in which God has worked to build his kingdom by means that have confounded all human expectations and displayed the divine freedom to act without the agency of either church or mission. Missionary history serves to illustrate the apostolic principle that, while we may be privileged to plant and water the seed of the Gospel, *it is God who makes it grow.* Paul's ringing affirmation of this principle serves to correct an activism that too easily slides into self-confidence and ignores the work of the Holy Spirit: 'So neither he who plants nor he who waters is anything, but only God, who makes things grow' (1 Cor. 3:6–7).

Consider the case of Christianity in China, which Western sinologists in the 1960s regarded as 'doomed to slowly die out' because of its 'ineradicable foreign connections' (Bays: 1996, vii). The expulsion of Western missionaries from China following the Communist revolution created a crisis of confidence for the missionary movement as a whole and there was anxiety in Europe and America concerning the viability of the Chinese church in this situation. And yet, thirty years later the unexpected had happened and scholars now talk of 'a flood of manifestations of the revival of religion, especially popular religion, which was nothing short of spectacular'. The number of Christians in China has grown tenfold since 1949 and has been conservatively estimated at between 20 to 30 million. Even more significant is the fact that Christianity has now become a clearly identifiable Chinese religion 'and part of the Chinese social scene' (*ibid.*: ix). Precisely in the absence of foreign missionaries, a process of genuine inculturation and translation took place which has resulted in the emergence of an independent Chinese church which, given the role that China seems destined to play on the world scene in the twenty-first century, is a phenomenon of incalculable significance.

Something very similar has happened in South America, where the extraordinary growth of an indigenous form of Pentecostal religion has taken Western theologians and social scientists by surprise. Harvey Cox concludes that this development may be part of a global movement which represents nothing short of the 'reshaping of religion in the twenty first century' (Cox: 1995). The British sociologist David Martin, who has himself made major contributions to the academic study of the processes of secularisation in the West, has testified that the encounter with Pentecostalism in South America revealed the short-comings of the theoretical models used within the sociology of religion. Scholarly assumptions concerning the inevitability of a growing and irreversible process of secularisation, which was believed to be the direct consequence of modernisation, have seriously narrowed the vision of Western academics. A theory which assumed the remorseless progress of secularisation had prevented its advocates from noticing, or at least, taking seriously, evidence that indicated not merely the survival of religion in the modern world, but its resurgence and growing social significance. Martin describes the conversion of 40 million Latin Americans to 'a genuinely indigenous version of Pentecostal and evangelical faith' as an event of epochal significance and one which exposes the inadequacy of the paradigms governing the study and teaching of the sociology of religion (Martin: 1999, 20).

What we are describing here is the emergence of *world Christianity*, the arrival of the church as a truly multicultural community. This development displays what Paul called 'the wisdom and knowledge of God' (Rom. 11:33) in that, as in the fruits of his own ministry among the Gentiles, the results of cross-cultural mission have taken everyone by surprise. The outcome of mission is *not* predictable and frequently confounds the human wisdom which imagines that it can anticipate and measure all things (1 Cor. 1:20). What is more, cross-cultural mission has *not* resulted in the expansion and reproduction of the missionary church, but has rather triggered responses to Christ from *within* a rich diversity of cultures. This in turn has led to the discovery of new aspects of the truth of Christ and to an enlarged awareness of the nature and significance of the church within God's purpose. This is precisely why Paul can claim that mission makes visible what would otherwise have remained hidden because through the church, in its glorious unity-in-diversity, 'the manifold wisdom of God' is shown to the rulers in the heavenly realms (Eph. 3:9–10). In Kenneth Cragg's words, the relationship of Christianity to the world is not merely geographical and expansionist, 'but integral and expectant'. The irrevocable call to go into all the world involves more than physical mobility because the apostolic affirmation that the Gospel is 'worthy of all acceptation' (1 Tim. 1:15) implies that a 'whole world is needed to apprehend a whole Christ and embrace a whole Church' (Cragg: 1968, 170–71). It is this which demands that Western Christians who have been socialised within the Christendom paradigm, undergo a *mental* change which, far from creating a sense of departure and loss, can bring liberation and an enlarged perception of the nature and purpose of the Christian mission.

At this point it is important to recognise that the changes to which reference is being made here point up the need for a process of *theological* renewal and transformation. As we have seen, paradigm shifts in the theology of mission have always resulted in the emergence of new and enlarged theological perspectives. We have traced just such a shift in our study of the experience of the apostle Peter at the cultural frontier between Jews and Gentiles in the first century and similar advances have occurred each time the Gospel seed has born fruit in new cultural and religious contexts. Kenneth Cragg, observing the boldness with which the apostolic church allowed certain key theological phrases, such as 'kingdom of heaven' and 'Son of man', to *lapse* and be replaced in the process of missionary translation, says that the lesson this teaches must not be lost on us today. If the principle of the translation of the Gospel, and the growth in the church's understanding of Christ as the direct outcome of this process, is embedded within the New Testament itself, then Christians are clearly guilty of unfaithfulness if, through timidity and fear, they refuse the further light which is certain to result from the emergence of world Christianity in the twenty-first century. As Cragg says,

> It is easy, for familiar reasons, to want the New Testament utterly innocent of the sort of vocabulary borrowing that might be perversely cited as syncretistic. But in that event it would not be the New Testament. The fear of syncretism, either as a charge then or a menace now, must not be allowed to obscure New Testament creativity of mind and usage or inhibit a present energy in the interpretation of Christ . . . For paralysis with dogma is always worse than risk for it. (Cragg: 1968, 57–8)

In this situation the church in the Western world faces both huge challenges and great opportunities. The challenges include the frank recognition that its assumed theological hegemony over the world church is at an end and the acceptance of the fact that the Western traditions represent more or less faithful, culturally conditioned responses to the revelation of God in Jesus Christ. Such recognition does *not* imply that the culture-conditioned aspect of these traditions is something to be ashamed of, since this is an unavoidable and inevitable outcome of the missionary implantation of the seed of the Gospel in this culture. In this process there were risks and losses, but also clear gains as the minds and hearts of people schooled in Greek philosophy and Roman law, or Renaissance humanism, or Enlightenment science, were surrendered to Christ and used in submission to his lordship. However, repentance is appropriate in relation to the arrogance that, from time to time, has led Western Christians to assume that their conceptual tools enabled them to define the *whole* meaning of Christ without remainder, so effectively imprisoning the Lord and Saviour of all cultures within the narrow confines of Western thought and social structures. Where attitudes like this persist and the light which the Lord has yet to 'break forth from his word' is refused, then great dangers lie in wait. Perhaps the greatest of these pitfalls is that, in the context of the world we have described in this book, Western Christianity runs a serious risk of becoming an ideology justifying a global system that stands under the judgement of God.

The Hispanic historian and theologian Justo Gonzalez has suggested that there is a remarkable parallel between the challenges facing world Christianity today and those which confronted John of Patmos at the end of the first century of the Christian era. Then as now, he observes, the cultural and ethnic encounters which occurred as peoples moved across the world did not take place 'in abstraction of economic and political systems'. Peoples did not (and do not) uproot themselves from their traditional lands and undertake perilous journeys to unknown regions out of a kind of wanderlust, but because of necessity: 'When the rivers of wealth flow in one direction, it is only natural for population to flow in the same direction (Gonzalez: 1999, 83). In precisely such a situation John of Patmos was summoned to prophesy to the churches '*about* many peoples and nations and languages and kings' (Rev. 10:11), imparting a fresh vision of the new humankind in which the Gentiles take their place alongside the tribes of Israel and together they become a kingdom of priests. For the prophet this vision is bittersweet 'because it involves radical change in the very congregations where John has served and which he loves'.

> And so it is with us today. The multicultural vision is sweet. But there is also a bitter side to it. There is the bitter side of having to declare that the vision of many peoples, many tribes, many nations, and many languages involves much more than bringing a bit of color and folklore

into our traditional services. It involves radical changes in the way we understand ourselves, and in the way we run our business.

(Gonzalez: 1999, 92)

There is another side to this particular coin and it concerns the missionary challenge represented by the Western world itself. In the course of the last decade, as the evidence of a massive recession from Christianity in Europe and, to a lesser extent, North America has become clear, increasing attention has been given to the need to develop 'missionary churches'. A plethora of books has appeared advocating 'seeker-friendly' services and proposing new models of the church adapted to meet the felt needs of postmodern people in cultures dominated by consumerism and entertainment. The crucial question to be raised with regard to such proposals concerns the extent to which they are based on a recognition of the true nature and extent of the *cultural* challenge involved in a missionary engagement with the contemporary Western world. Sadly, many such proposals for the renewal of the churches in mission betray lurking assumptions that, if a surface-level hostility toward traditional religion can be overcome, contemporary people remain basically hospitable and friendly to the message of Christ. Mission is thus understood, like almost everything else in this culture, as a matter of appropriate, effective and highly professional presentation, or more accurately, marketing. Here again, I suggest, Western Christians need to experience a mental, conceptual and spiritual transformation. In this case, received ideas concerning evangelism, which are based on Christendom assumptions that the church and the world share a basically common world-view, simply will no longer do. More than thirty years ago a European theologian demolished the assumption that evangelism could appeal to something that lay dormant in the memories of secular people, as though there was a residue of the Christian message still buried somewhere in the consciousness of the masses. Such presuppositions, he said, will have to be abandoned:

> There is nothing left that can be called into memory, nothing that can be awakened. What still might be present as 'residue' is usually only some sort of forced image of a caricature Christendom. With that, one has become immune to the real thing... All this is to say that the apostolate in a post-Christian situation will have to lose all semblance of a 'revival movement' and will have to bear the signature of *mission work*. (Hoekendijk: 1967, 50)

At this point I want to suggest that the churches in the Western world would do well to consider carefully the lessons to be found in the records of previous attempts to transmit the message of the Gospel across cultural barriers. In other words, the *history of mission* is full of instruction, including both negative and positive examples, which can be of enormous assistance to churches confronting the daunting challenge of cross-culturation at the frontiers we have described in this book.

For example, a church confronting a world that lives *after* Christendom might anticipate discovering useful parallels and principles in the experience of the church that existed *before* Christendom. The two contexts are not the same of course, but there are clear similarities and the further Christendom recedes in our rear-view mirrors, the more relevant the experiences of the fathers of the church will be found to be. The Christians we encounter in this period have a deep awareness of the radical nature of conversion and the moral demands of Christian discipleship. In the second century, Justin Martyr speaks of a desperate struggle to get free from a world controlled by demons, a culture in which people are *addicted* to wealth and pleasure, and describes the new life in Christ in terms of a complete transformation:

> Those who once rejoiced in fornication now delight in self-control alone . . . We who once took most pleasure in the means of increasing our wealth and property now bring what we have into a common fund and share with everyone in need; we who hated and killed one another and would not associate with men of different tribes . . . now . . . live together and pray for our enemies . . .
>
> (Bradstock and Rowland [eds]: 2002, 2)

Little wonder that we later discover Cyprian marvelling at the countercultural qualities displayed in the lives of Christians and asking himself how such conversions could be possible. How could the Graeco-Roman values and affections which were 'so deeply and radically ingrained within us' ever be dislodged and replaced? Where, he asks, does a man learn to live a sober and contented life when his entire existence has been characterised by 'liberal banquets' and sumptuous feasts? He found the answer when 'by the help of the water of new birth' the stain of the old life was washed away, a 'light from above, serene and pure' was infused into his heart, and the Spirit breathed from heaven, granting a second birth which 'restored me to a new person' (*ibid.*: 3). When accounts like these are placed alongside the analysis of the culture of economism offered in this book, their dynamic relevance becomes obvious, even as they expose the inadequacy of our understanding of conversion and discipleship. At the conclusion of a brilliant study of the nature of Christian conversion in the early church, Alan Kreider asks what it would mean for the churches today to insist on biblical standards of regeneration and transformation. He comments:

> What if our churches' initiatory rites – as the globe warms and the ecological crisis intensifies – baptized people into communities of brothers and sisters who feast at the table of Christ's sufficiency? What if these churches were known as communities of contentment and compassion? . . . Such churches, having learned from the past, would have something authentic to contribute to the future.
>
> (Kreider: 1999, 107)

Actually, help may also be discovered from other sources much nearer to home. For Christians throughout central and eastern Europe, the end of Christendom occurred decades ago in circumstances that compelled urgent and unavoidable theological reflection on the true nature and calling of the churches. Janos Pasztor, a Hungarian theologian, looks back on the experience of believers during the era of Communist domination and says that important lessons were learned then that cannot be abandoned 'without serious loss to our future orientation'. It was, he says, when all the traditional supports and privileges enjoyed by Christians in the past were withdrawn, and a militant form of materialist philosophy began to shape the social sphere and control the system of education, in this context faith *revived* as 'the meaning of life was granted to us in Christ in a climate of false meanings and meaninglessness' (Pasztor: 1995, 22).

It is in experiences of this kind that the *missio Dei* – the 'mission of God' – becomes visible in human history as the divine wisdom confounds human intentions and expectations. According to Pasztor, the Communist obssession with the material basis of life resulted in a narrowing of vision which prevented those in power from being able to recognise the transforming effect of the word of God. As we have noted earlier, a similar renewal occurred in Czechoslovakia, in which, amid 'deeply shattered Christian institutions', the Christian life suddenly became again a *narrow way* and the churches found themselves gifted an opportunity to achieve fresh credibility (Lochman: 1988, 18). The relevance of all this to our struggle today to discover new forms of missionary obedience in an emerging pluralist society is recognised by Janos Pasztor:

> The most important lesson to be learned from the 'theology of the serving church' is to deepen the christological basis of our faith, and to build ecclesiology and church life in practice upon it. This will help us avoid the temptations of either triumphalism or despair, and thus to find our role and mission among the great crises of humankind as we face the third millennium. (Pasztor: 1995, 35)

Christ and the Religions

Despite the remarkable growth of world Christianity, the fact remains that the other religions have not been displaced as a result of this advance. On the contrary, there is considerable evidence to suggest that they are increasingly resurgent, both within their traditional heartlands and, in the age of globalisation, as missionary faiths offering spiritual solace to people in the secularised Western world. In other words, contemporary religious pluralism presents a massive challenge to Christian mission, as indicated by the sober historical judgement of Jaroslav Pelikan:

> Despite the phenomenal success of Christian missions during the nineteenth and twentieth centuries, it seems incontestable that the percentage of Christians in the total world population is continually declining, and therefore it seems inconceivable that the Christian church and the Christian message will ever conquer the population of the world and replace the other religions of the human race. If Jesus is to become the Man Who Belongs to the World, it will have to be by some other way. (Pelikan: 1985, 230)

As we seek to discover what this 'other way' might be, our starting point must be the conclusion to which these studies clearly point, that a 'conquest' model of mission which anticipates the *replacement* of other cultural and religious traditions by the form of Christianity known to the missionaries *is inconsistent with the apostolic example found on the pages of the New Testament*. More than thirty years ago Kenneth Cragg wrote that Christianity must be ready to 'die to the possessiveness of western forms in order to live authentically within the fullness of human cultures' (Cragg: 1968, 193). The truth of this statement has already been illustrated in our discussion of world Christianity in the previous section, but now the question arises as to whether this principle might point us toward the 'other way', in which Christ may increasingly become the 'Man Who Belongs to the World'. If the outcome of mission at the beginning of the first millennium was that Jesus of Nazareth became the Christ of Athens and Rome (with all that was involved in that momentous development), must we not face the challenge of ensuring that, through a similar process of translation and inculturation in the third millennium, the Christ so long associated with Europe and North America becomes the Christ of the whole world? Cragg's observation that Jesus is only truly known in his fullness 'when the whole world, in its cultural diversity takes possession of Him and in freedom, in thought and form, tells of Him what it learns and loves' is a profoundly apostolic and biblical insight (*ibid.*: 195). What is more, non-Western Christians who follow Jesus in contexts of radical religious pluralism in which their faith places them at the margins of societies dominated by ancient and revered traditions, insist that the credibility of the Gospel depends upon the separation of Christ from modern, secular values. Thus, Chee Pang Choong, a theologian based in Singapore and visiting professor at the University of Beijing, says, 'For years I have been trying very hard to convince my part of the world that it is a very serious mistake or misunderstanding to identify the West with Christianity without much qualification'. Moreover, Professor Choong insists that far from being simply an Asian concern, in the era of globalisation this is an issue with 'profound implications for the life and mission of the church' (Choong: 1999, 364–5).

But how is this to come about? What shape will the post-Christendom paradigm of mission take, particularly in relation to the religions of the world? If Christ is to be known and recognised as the atoning sacrifice not only for 'our sins', but also 'for the sins of the whole world' (1 John 2:2), what changes are required in missionary theology and practice? I suggest that the first priority involves the recovery of the *biblical pattern of conversion* which we discovered in the study of the Peter and Cornelius narrative in Chapter 5 of this book. Andrew Walls has pointed out that there is a clear distinction between proselytism and conversion throughout the New Testament. Prior to the coming of Christ the Jewish people possessed a well-established process by means of which devout and God-seeking Gentiles might be admitted to the community of Israel. They underwent the rite of circumcision, were immersed in water and were systematically instructed in the Law of Moses. They were, in other words, effectively de-cultured as Gentiles and received into the community as *proselytes*; that is to say, to all outward appearances they became Jewish. The early church was of course familiar with this model but, amazingly, set it aside in favour of a new approach involving *conversion*. The story told in the book of Acts charts this extraordinary movement which involved a clear break with Jewish tradition and led to a situation in which Gentile converts to Christ were 'left to find a Christian lifestyle of their own within Hellenistic society under the guidance of the Holy Spirit'. Christian converts, in contrast to Jewish proselytes, were not to be extracted from their culture; they were quite explicitly to remain within Greek society and to evolve a pattern of discipleship within that context. In fact, says Andrew Walls,

> ... it was their task as converts to convert their society; convert it in the sense that they had to learn to keep turning their ways of thinking and doing things – which, of course, were Greek ways of thinking and doing things – towards Christ, opening them up to his influence. In this way a truly Greek, truly Hellenistic type of Christianity was able to emerge. (Walls: 1999, 387)

The implications of this are simply enormous. In practice Christian missions have usually employed the language of *conversion* while actually requiring people from other cultures and religions to become *proselytes*. The apostolic boldness in declining to impose on converts more than the core demands of faith and discipleship (a principle for which Paul contends throughout his letters) has rarely been imitated. Like the Judaisers in the New Testament, faced with the apparent high risks involved when working among 'pagans', Christians have usually failed to exercise a radical trust in the Holy Spirit and instead have imposed on 'converts' pre-packaged forms of church life and discipleship which have extracted them from their society, isolated them from their own communities and rendered them powerless to bear witness to Christ from the *inside* of their own cultures. There is evidence to suggest that cross-cultural missionaries being sent from churches in the southern hemisphere today are repeating this mistake, seeking proselytes rather than converts within non-Christian cultures and religions (in the year AD 2000 an estimated 6,800 Korean Christians were at work in other countries of the world).

In considering what a 'conversion' model of mission might look like in practice I want to refer to a remarkable account of a movement toward Christ from *within* Islam. Malam Ibrahim was a devout Islamic scholar who became convinced of the supreme importance of the prophet *Isa* (Jesus) as the result of his studies of the *Qu'ran*. Ibrahim had no contact with Western Christianity or its missionary representatives, and no access to the New Testament, yet he determined to make a systematic study of every reference to Jesus in the *Qu'ran* (Crampton: 1975, 129). This study led him to believe that *Isa* was 'greater than all' and was to be revered and followed. So convinced was he of this that he began sharing his discoveries with fellow Muslims in the northern Nigerian city of Kano and gathered a group of followers around him who became known as *Isawa* – followers of Jesus. Almost inevitably the group attracted the attention of the Emir and Ibrahim was arrested, tried and executed by being impaled on a stake in Kano market. Yet the *Isawa* survived – a group of Muslims devoted to Jesus and inspired in that devotion by a prophetic leader whose own death so clearly reflected that of the Christ he had dimly known, yet faithfully followed.

The question which this account poses for both Western missions and non-Western churches is this: if the figure of Malam Ibrahim stands before us as a contemporary 'Cornelius', are we able to affirm that such evidence of the work of God's grace *within* the religions convinces us, as it did the apostle Peter, that 'God does not show favouritism but accepts men from every nation who fear him and do what is right' (Acts 10:34)? And are we able to imitate Peter's missiological and pastoral response in such a situation, trusting the Holy Spirit in such a manner that our urge to *proselytise* such individuals and movements is overcome, so avoiding the implication that following Jesus as Lord means *becoming like us*? Questions like these are critical on the frontier of pluralisation because devout adherents of other faiths are unlikely ever to get close to the Jesus of the Gospels as long as the lifestyle of evangelists, or the worship of churches shaped by Western individualism and modernisation, makes him appear to be the destroyer of all that is treasured within their traditions. The tragedy of the proselytising approach to mission is that it turns the Gospel into 'bad news', ensures the closing of ranks, and short-circuits the revolutionary impact of the living Christ within these religious traditions. What is more, it ignores the profound insight of John of Patmos that *all* the peoples on earth may bring their 'glory and honour' *into* the kingdom of God (Rev. 21:26).

At this point this book has come almost full circle as the frontiers we have discussed begin to merge together to form a single horizon. The distinction we have just made between proselytism and conversion is of vital importance, I suggest, not only at the frontier of religious *pluralisation*, but also at the frontiers of *secularisation* and *globalis-*

ation. A postmodern generation displaying a growing sense of spiritual hunger, needs to encounter the life-changing Christ in a way that does not require the acceptance of ecclesiastical baggage from the past, but allows freedom, under the guidance of the Holy Spirit, to turn contemporary processes of thought and ways of living towards the Saviour. In this way, *and only in this way,* the economistic culture we have described in Chapter 6 might be converted and transformed with consequences for the future of the world that can scarcely be imagined at the present time. Moreover, the frontiers of mission we have described will be found to overlap and intertwine, since, as the sociologist David Lyon puts it, in a globalising world 'the cross may turn out to have more in common with the crescent than with the swoosh or the golden arches' (Lyon: 2002, 89).

Structures and Strategies

In the first chapter of this book we discussed the crisis facing Western missionary agencies at a time of massive social and cultural change. You will recall the question asked by Max Warren as to whether we have reached the end of the modern missionary age 'in any shape recognizably continuous with the past'. The one thing that can be said with a degree of certainty in responding to this question is that Western missionary organisations which ignore the implications of the emerging frontiers described in this book are unlikely to survive long into the twenty-first century. However, while it is not my purpose to suggest the nature of the institutional change and restructuring which this context demands, I do want to propose that organisations with leadership able to turn them towards the new frontiers may yet make a vital contribution to the missionary calling of the people of God.

Consider this possible scenario of the world in 2025. The northern hemisphere is populated by people who are incredibly wealthy, yet find it increasingly difficult to articulate the meaning of human existence in any coherent or rational manner. While the material prosperity of these people continues to grow, their numbers are in decline as birth rates in Europe and North America fall. Meanwhile, 'this future North confronts the poorer and vastly more numerous global masses who wave flags not of red revolution, but of ascendant Christianity and Islam' (Jenkins: 2002, 161). The Islamic and Hindu resurgences have continued but, alongside them, the 'Third Church' has also grown at a phenomenal rate so that there are now huge Christian communities in countries like

Brazil, Mexico, Nigeria, Korea, the Philippines and China. These churches are unlike those which still exist in the North in two crucial respects. First, they are overwhelmingly charismatic and conservative in character, reading the New Testament in ways that seem puzzlingly literal to their friends in the North. Second, they are churches largely made up of poor people who in many cases live on the very edge of existence. Philip Jenkins suggests that in this scenario, we in the West may come to be viewed as 'the final Babylon' – perhaps in the light of this study *we already are!*

In such a context, which is very far from being a fanciful vision, Northern politicians, intellectuals and journalists will find themselves confronting a world increasingly shaped by a form of religion they simply cannot comprehend. As Jenkins says:

> As Northern media come to recognize the growing importance of the Southern states, and seek to explain their values, it is all too likely that Southern Christianity will be interpreted through the same kind of racial and cultural stereotypes that have so often been applied to fundamentalist or enthusiastic religion ... The Christian faith of the rising states, we will probably hear, is fanatical, superstitious, demagogic: it is politically reactionary and sexually repressive. (*ibid.*)

What might the role of Western missions be in this scenario? Mission organisations would find themselves increasingly located between two worlds, in which, on the one hand, they identified with the cries coming from their sisters and brothers in the South, while, on the other hand, they would be called to play a mediating role between that world and the one within which they operate. Jenkins suggests that as these two worlds drift apart there is a possibility that the secular and fabulously wealthy North will increasingly view the faith of one third of the human race as threatening and dangerous and so would end up *defining itself against Christianity* (*ibid.*: 162). The task of the churches in the North in this situation is clear: faithfulness to Christ would demand that they became increasingly counter-cultural while offering a consistent, unflinching challenge to the stereotyping and misrepresentation of Southern Christianity, whether this comes from government briefings or media images. In addition, a missionary church would bear costly witness to the fact that the deep spiritual sickness afflicting the rich North might actually be healed when the voices from the other world are heard and understood. It is not difficult to see that in a context like this missionary organisations possessing the experience and wisdom gained from two centuries of work in cross-cultural locations would be uniquely placed to contribute to the healing of the wounds of the world through a movement of globalisation from below.

There remains, however, the stubborn challenge of missionary witness to people of other faiths. In the scenario we have described, resurgent Islam as well as Southern Christianity is set over against the crass materialism and existential emptiness of the rich North. This means that while the line dividing North from South would be of critical significance, there would be other points of tension between the religions, where different understandings of God, or revelation, or salvation, may lead to violent conflict. Thus, if missions have a continuing role in facilitating short-term cross-cultural experience and learning for a maximum number of young people, I want to argue that they must also retain a commitment to the training and support of people with a calling to the life-long process of gaining a profound understanding of other religions and engagement in missionary conversation with people belonging to those faiths. In this sense, although one long-established paradigm of mission is fading, the great challenge of fulfilling the missionary calling of the people of God remains. As Max Warren himself recognised, writing to his son-in-law who was engaged in missionary dialogue with Hinduism:

> For my part I am in no kind of despair. I find this a most exciting moment to be alive. I want to fill what days remain to my lot to help folk to recover some basic certainties & then be ready to explore how to relate these certainties to a new world & a new age. The great days of mission lie ahead – Hallelujah! (Kings: 2002, 211)

The Abiding Presence

I want to end this book with a final visit to the art gallery. The modern French painter Georges Rouault has been described as one of the most singular figures in the history of twentieth-century art. A contemporary of Henri Matisse, he turned his attention to the study of human misery, painting working-class people, clowns, prostitutes and other folk at the margins of modern society. His many depictions of circus people are unforgettable, contrasting the external jollity related to masks and costumes with the profound inner sadness of the life concealed behind the professional disguise. Rouault wrote: 'Later on, I clearly realized that the clown was myself, he was all of us, almost all of us' (Faerna:

n.d., 18). Throughout his life Rouault retained strong religious convictions and was a close friend of the Catholic philosopher Jacques Maritain. However, religion was not for Rouault a means of escape from the world, rather it moved him to depict the sorrow and suffering of human beings in all its stark reality. The incarnate Christ identified himself with the poor and hopeless and so Rouault painted Jesus as the 'poor Saviour of the poor'. In a work entitled *Christ in the Outskirts* (picture 10) he depicts Jesus beside two poor children in a desolate city street. The term 'outskirts' is misleading since it carries connotations of suburbia and the bourgeois society which the artist despised; 'slums' might be more accurate, highlighting Rouault's conviction that Christ is to be discovered in the most desolate of places on earth where he brings hope and comfort to those on the underside of society.

I am reminded of the words of the Dutch missionary theologian Johannes Verkuyl, who wrote that Christ promises to be with his church during 'all of her days' (Matt. 28:20). However, he said, 'the church must forever be asking "What kind of day is it today?", for no two days are alike in her history'. The days and ages change, yet as the church carries on her mission in the six continents, one fact never changes: 'Jesus Christ is urging on his church to complete her missionary calling as he guides her to her final destination' (Verkuyl: 1978, 108).

This book has been an attempt to describe 'what kind of day it is today'.

Bibliography

Ambler, Rex. 1999 'The Self and Postmodernity' in Flanagan and Jupp (eds), pp.134–51

Bainton, Roland H. 1972 *Erasmus of Christendom* (London: Collins/Fontana)

Bauckham, Richard. 1993(a) *The Climax of Prophecy: Studies on the Book of Revelation* (Edinburgh: T & T Clark)

    1993(b) *The Theology of the Book of Revelation* (Cambridge: Cambridge University Press)

Bauman, Zygmunt. 1992 *Mortality, Immortality and Other Life Strategies* (Cambridge: Polity Press)

    1997 *Postmodernity and its Discontents* (Cambridge: Polity Press)

    1998 *Globalization: The Human Consequences* (Cambridge: Polity Press)

Bavinck, J. H. 1981 *The Church Between Temple and Mosque: A Study of the Relationship Between the Christian Faith and Other Religions* (Grand Rapids: Eerdmans)

Bays, Daniel H. (ed). 1996 *Christianity in China: From the Eighteenth Century to the Present* (Stanford: Stanford University Press)

Beck, Ulrich. 2000 *What is Globalization?* (Cambridge: Polity Press)

Berdyaev, Nicholas. 1935 *The Fate of Man in the Modern World* (London: SCM Press)

Berger, John. 1998 'Against the Great Defeat of the World', *Race & Class* 40/2–3, October, pp.1–4

Berger, Peter. 1961 *The Noise of Solemn Assemblies* (Garden City, NY: Doubleday)

    1979 *The Heretical Imperative: Contemporary Possibilities of Religious Affirmation* (Garden City, NY: Anchor Press/Doubleday)

Boer, Jan H. 1984 *Missions: Heralds of Christ or Capitalism?* (Ibadan: Daystar Press)

Bonhoeffer, Dietrich. 1970 *No Rusty Swords: letters, lectures and notes, 1928–1936,* from *The Collected Works,* ed. Edwin Robertson (London: Collins/Fontana)

Bonk, Jonathan J. 1989 'Missions and Mammon: Six Theses', *International Bulletin of Missionary Research,* 13/3, pp.169–176

    1998 *Missions and Money: Affluence as a Western Missionary Problem* (New York: Orbis Books)

Bosch, D. J. 1977 *Missiology and Science of Religion* [Study Guide for Course MSR303] (Pretoria: University of South Africa)

Bosch, David. 1991 *Transforming Mission: Paradigm Shifts in the Theology of Mission* (New York: Orbis Books)

Boyle, Nicholas. 1998 *Who Are We Now? Christian Humanism and the Global Market from Hegel to Heaney* (Edinburgh: T&T Clark)

Bradstock, Andrew and Rowland, Christopher (eds). 2002 *Radical Christian Writings: A Reader* (Oxford: Blackwell)

Brenon, Anne. 1997 'Heresies in the Middle Ages: "There are Two Churches"', *Concilium* [eds: Guiseppe Ruggieri and Miklos Tomka], 1997/3, pp.63–70

135

Brierley, Peter. 2000 *The Tide is Running Out* (London: Christian Research)

Bright, John. 1976 *Covenant and Promise: The Prophetic Understanding of the Future in Pre-Exilic Israel* (Philadelphia: Westminster Press)

Brown, Callum. 2001 *The Death of Christian Britain: Understanding Secularisation, 1800–2000* (London: Routledge)

Brueggemann, Walter. 1978 *The Prophetic Imagination* (Philadelphia: Fortress Press)

1986 *Hopeful Imagination: Prophetic Voices in Exile* (Philadelphia: Fortress Press)

1987 *Hope Within History* (Atlanta: John Knox Press)

(ed). 2001 *Hope for the World: Mission in a Global Context* (Louisville: Westminster/John Knox Press)

Brueggemann, Walter and Stroup, George W. (eds). *Many Voices, One God: Being Faithful in a Pluralistic World* (Louisville: Westminster/John Knox Press)

Bühlmann, Walbert. 1982 *God's Chosen Peoples* (New York: Orbis Books)

Calvin, John. 1960 [1546] *The First Epistle of Paul the Apostle to the Corinthians*, translated by John W. Fraser (London/Edinburgh: Oliver & Boyd)

1965 [1560] *The Acts of the Apostles, 1–13*, translated by John Fraser and W.J.G. McDonald (Edinburgh/London: Oliver & Boyd)

Carey, William. 1801 *Periodical Accounts Relative to A Society Formed Among The Particular Baptists for the Propogating of the Gospel Among the Heathen, Volume II* [no details]

Carroll, John. 1993 *Humanism: The Wreck of Human Culture* (London: Collins/Fontana)

1998 *Ego and Soul: The Modern West In Search of Meaning* (Sydney: Harper/Collins)

Chang, Curtis. 2000 *Engaging Unbelief: A Captivating Strategy from Augustine & Aquinas* (Downers Grove/Leicester: Apollos)

Choong Chee Pang. 1999 'A Friendly Observer's View of North American Global Mission Responsibility Today' in Martinson, Paul Varo (ed), *Mission at the Dawn of the 21st Century* (Minneapolis: Kirk House Publishing), pp.368–9

Cocker, Mark. 1999 *Rivers of Blood, Rivers of Gold: Europe's Conflict with Tribal Peoples* (London: Pimlico)

Collier, Jane and Esteban, Rafael. 1998 *From Complicity to Encounter: The Church and the Culture of Economism* (Harrisburg: Trinity Press International)

Costas, Orlando E. 1984 *Christ Outside the Gate: Mission Beyond Christendom* (New York: Orbis Books)

Coupland, Douglas. 1994 *Life After God* (London: Touchstone Books)

Cox, Harvey. 1995 *Fire From Heaven: The Rise of Pentecostal Spirituality and the Reshaping of Religion in the Twenty-First Century* (Reading, Mass.: Addison-Wesley)

Cracknell, Kenneth. 1995 *Justice, Courtesy and Love: Theologians and Missionaries Encountering World Religions, 1846–1914* (London: Epworth Press)

Cragg, Kenneth. 1968 *Christianity in World Perspective* (London: Lutterworth Press)

1992 *Troubled by Truth: Life-Studies in Inter-Faith Concern* (Durham: Pentland Press)

1998 *The Secular Experience of God* (Harrisburg/Leominster: Trinity Press International/Gracewing Publishers)

Crampton, E.P.T. 1975 *Christianity in Northern Nigeria* (London: Geoffrey Chapman)

Davie, Grace. 2002 *Europe: The Exceptional Case* (London: Darton Longman & Todd)

Delitzsch, Franz. 1960 [1877] *Biblical Commentary on the Prophecies of Isaiah Volume I* (Grand Rapids: Eerdmans)

Descartes, René. 1968 *Discourse on Method and the Meditations* (Harmondsworth: Penguin Books)

Dostoevsky, Fyodor. 1955 *The Idiot* (Harmondsworth: Penguin Books)

Dussel, Enrique. 1990 'The Real Motives for the Conquest' in Boff, Leonardo and Elizondo, Virgil (eds), *1492–1992: The Voice of the Victims* (London: SCM Press [Concilium Special]), pp.30–46

Ellul, Jacques. 1986 *The Subversion of Christianity* (Grand Rapids: Eerdmans)

Engel, James F. and Dyrness, William A. 2000 *Changing the Mind of Missions: Where Have We Gone Wrong?* (Downers Grove: Inter Varsity Press)

Escobar, Samuel. 1994 'Mission in the New World Order', *Prism*, January, pp.16–21
2000 'The Global Scenario at the Turn of the Century' in Taylor, William D. (ed), pp.24–46

Faerna, Jose Maria (ed). n.d. *Great Modern Masters: Rouault* (New York: Cameo/Abrams)

Fernando, Ajith. 1999 *An Authentic Servant* (Singapore: OMF International)

Flanagan, Kieran and Jupp, Peter (eds). 1999 *Postmodernity, Sociology and Religion*, 2nd ed. (London/New York: Macmillan/St Martin's Press)

Fletcher, Richard. 1997 *The Barbarian Conversion* (New York: Henry Holt)

Foster, John. 1945 *World Church* (London: SCM Press)

Frank, Thomas. 2001 *One Market Under God: Extreme Capitalism, Market Populism, and the End of Economic Democracy* (London: Secker & Warburg)

Gibson, Walter S. 1973 *Hieronymus Bosch* (London: Thames & Hudson)

Gonzalez, Justo J. 1999 *For the Healing of the Nations: The Book of Revelation in an Age of Cultural Conflict* (New York: Orbis Books)

Goudzwaard, Bob. 1997 *Capitalism and Progress: A Diagnosis of Western Society* (Carlisle: Paternoster Publishing)

Guder, Darrell L. 2000 *The Continuing Conversion of the Church* (Grand Rapids: Eerdmans)

Hall, Douglas John. 1985 *Christian Mission: The Stewardship of Life in the Kingdom of Death* (New York: Friendship Press)
1998 'Confessing Christ in a Religiously Plural Context' in Brueggemann, Walter and Stroup, George (eds), pp.65–77

Hauerwas, Stanley and Willimon, William. 1989 *Resident Aliens* (Nashville: Abingdon Press)

Hiebert, Paul G. 1999 *Missiological Implications of Epistemological Shifts* (Harrisburg: Trinity Press International)

Hobsbawm, Eric. 1995 *Age of Extremes: The Short Twentieth Century, 1914–1991* (London: Abacus)

Hoekendijk, J.C. 1967 *The Church Inside Out* (London: SCM Press)

Horst, Willis G. 2001 'Spirituality of the Toba/Qom Christians of the Argentine Chaco', *Missiology*, XXIX/2, April, pp.165–84

Huntington, Samuel P. 1993 'The Clash of Civilizations?', *Foreign Affairs*, Summer, pp.22–49
1998 *The Clash of Civilizations and the Remaking of World Order* (London/New York: Touchstone Books)

Ignatieff, Michael. 1999 'The Ascent of Man?' in *BBC Proms '99* (London: BBC Publications)

Jenkins, Philip. 2002 *The Next Christendom: The Coming of Global Christianity* (Oxford/New York: Oxford University Press)

Johnstone, Patrick. 1998 *The Church is Bigger Than You Think* (Fearn, Rosshire: Christian Focus Publications)

Kempis, Thomas à. 1952 *The Imitation of Christ* (Harmondsworth: Penguin Books)

137

Kings, Graham. 2002 *Christianity Connected: Hindus, Muslims and the World in the Letters of Max Warren and Roger Hooker* (Zoetermeer, The Netherlands: Boekencentrum)

Klein, Naomi. 2000 *No Logo* (London: Flamingo/HarperCollins)

Köstenberger, Andreas and O'Brien, Peter. 2001 *Salvation to the Ends of the Earth: A Biblical Theology of Mission* (Leicester/Downers Grove: Apollos/Inter Varsity Press)

Kraus, C. Norman. 1998 *An Intrusive Gospel? Christian Mission in the Postmodern World* (Downers Grove: Inter Varsity Press)

Kreider, Alan. 1999 *The Change of Conversion and the Origin of Christendom* (Harrisburg: Trinity International Press)

Kundnani, Arun. 1998/99 'Where do you want to go today? The rise of information Capital', *Race & Class*, 40/2–3, October, pp.49–71

Küng, Hans. 1995 *Christianity – Its Essence and History* (London: SCM Press)

Lakeland, Paul. 1997 *Postmodernity: Christian Identity in a Fragmented Age* (Minneapolis: Fortress Press)

Lamb, C. A. 1982 *Jesus Through Other Eyes: Christology in Multi-Faith Context* (Oxford: Latimer House)

Lambert, Malcolm. 1998 *The Cathars* (Oxford: Blackwell)

Las Casas, Bartholomew de. 1992 [1542] *A Short Account of the Destruction of the Indies* (Harmondsworth: Penguin Books)

Latourette, Kenneth Scott. 1936 *Missions Tomorrow* (New York/London: Harper Brothers)

    1970 *A History of the Expansion of Christianity, Volume IV – The Great Century in Europe and the United States of America, AD1800–AD1914* (Grand Rapids: Zondervan)

Léry, Jean de. 1990 [1580] *A History of a Voyage To The Land of Brazil, Otherwise Called America*, translated and with Introduction by Janet Whatley (Berkeley/Los Angeles/Oxford: University of California Press)

Lochman, Jan Milic. 1988 *Christ and Prometheus?* (Geneva: WCC Publications)

Lyon, David. 2002 'Religion and Globalization' in Christopher Partridge (ed), *Dictionary of Contemporary Religion in the Western World* (Leicester: Inter Varsity Press), pp.85–9

MacDonald, J. I. 1910 *Foreign Missions and the Second Advent* (London: Morgan and Scott)

MacGregor, Neil. 2000 *The Image of Christ* (London: National Gallery)

Martin, David. 1969 *The Religious and the Secular: Studies in Secularization* (London: Routledge & Kegan Paul)

    1999 'Christian Foundations, Sociological Fundamentals', in Francis, Leslie (ed), *Sociology, Theology and the Curriculum* (London/New York: Cassell), pp.1–49

    2002 *Pentecostalism: The World Their Parish* (Oxford: Blackwell)

Martinson, Paul Varo (ed). 1999 *Mission at the Dawn of the 21st Century: A Vision for the Church* (Minneapolis: Kirk House Publishers)

Mead, Loren B. 1988 *The Once and Future Church: Reinventing the Church for a New Missionary Frontier* (New York: Alban Institute)

Miall, Edward. 1849 *The British Chuches in Relation to the British People* (London: Arthur Hall and Virtue)

Montgomery, Jim. 1997 *Then The End Will Come* (Pasadena: William Carey Library)

Murphy, Ronald G. 1989 *The Saxon Savior: The Germanic Transformation of the Gospel in the Ninth-Century Heliand* (New York/Oxford: Oxford University Press)

Newbigin, Lesslie. 1961 *A Faith for this One World?* (London: SCM Press)

    1984 *The Other Side of 1984* (Geneva: WCC)

Padilla, René. 1985 *Mission Between The Times* (Grand Rapids: Eerdmans)

    2001 'Mission at the Turn of the Century/Millennium', *Evangel*, Spring, pp.6–12

Padwick, Constance E. 1961 *Muslim Devotions: A Study of Prayer Manuals in Common Use* (London: SPCK)

Pannenberg, Wolfhart. 1988 *Christianity in a Secularized World* (London: SCM Press)

Pascal, Blaise. 1966 *Pensées* (Harmondsworth: Penguin Books)

Pasztor, Janos. 1995 'The Theology of the Serving Church and the Theology of Diaconia in the Protestant Churches and Their Consequences in Hungary During the Time of Socialism'. *Religion in Eastern Europe*, XV/6, pp.22–35

    2001 'The Church in the Context of Central Europe' in Brueggemann, Walter (ed), *Hope for the World: Mission in a Global Context* (Louisville: Westminster/John Knox Press), pp.51–3

Patience, Allan. 1999 'Is There a Theology of Globalisation?', *Zadok Perspectives*, 64, Winter, pp.242–3

Pelikan, Jaroslav. 1985 *Jesus Through The Centuries: His Place in the History of Culture* (New York: Harper & Row)

Peterson, Eugene H. 1993 *The Message – The New Testament in Contemporary Language* (Colorado Springs: Navpress)

Rabb, T. K. 1975 *The Struggle for Stability in Early Modern Europe* (New York: Oxford University Press)

Richard, Pablo. 1990 '1492: The Violence of God and the Future of Christianity' in Boff, Leonardo and Elizondo, Virgil (eds), *1492–1992: The Voice of the Victims* (London: SCM Press [Concilium Special]), pp.59–67

Richards, Glyn (ed). 1985 *A Source Book of Modern Hinduism* (London/Dublin: Curzon Press)

Richardson, Don. 1981 *Eternity in Their Hearts* (Ventura,California: Regal Books)

Rivera, Luis. 1992 *A Violent Evangelism: The Political and Religious Conquest of the Americas* (Louisville: Westminster/John Knox Press)

Roquebert, Michel. n.d. *Cathar Religion* (Toulouse: Editions Loubatières)

Rowland, Christopher. 2000 'A Community Which Hears the Apocalypse', in Yates, Timothy (ed), pp.9–17

Roxburgh, Alan. 1997 *The Missionary Congregation, Leadership and Liminality* (Harrisburg: Trinity Press International)

Roy, Arundhati. 2001 *The Reincarnation of Rumpelstiltskin*, www.zmag.org/roy.htm

Ruskin, John. 1997 [1862] *Unto This Last and Other Writings*, edited and with Introduction by Clive Wilmer (London: Penguin Books)

Sampson, Philip, Samuel, Vinay and Sugden, Chris (eds). 1994 *Faith and Modernity* (Oxford: Regnum Books/Lynx Communications)

Sanneh, Lamin. 1983 *West African Christianity; The Religious Impact* (New York: Orbis Books)

    1987 'Christian Missions and the Western Guilt Complex', *The Christian Century*, 8/April, pp.330–34

    1990 *Translating the Message: The Missionary Impact on Culture* (New York: Orbis Books)

    1993 *Encountering The West: Christianity and the Global Cultural Process, The African Dimension* (London: Marshall Pickering)

Schaeffer, Francis. 1969 *Death In The City* (London: Inter Varsity Press)

    1970 *The Church at the End of the Twentieth Century* (London: The Norfolk Press)

Seabrook, Jeremy. 1988 *The Race for Riches* (Basingstoke: Marshall Pickering)

Seel, John. 1994 'Modernity and evangelicals: American evangelicalism as a global case study' in Sampson, Samuel, Sugden (eds), pp.287–313

Senior, Donald and Stuhlmueller, Carroll. 1983 *The Biblical Foundations for Mission* (London: SCM Press)

Shenk, Wilbert R. 1999 *Changing Frontiers of Mission* (New York: Orbis Books)

Smith, David. 1989 'Church and Society in Britain: A Mid-Nineteenth Century Analysis by Edward Miall', *The Evangelical Quarterly*, LXI/2, April, pp.139–58

    1995 *Stairways To Heaven? God in World Religions* (Edinburgh: Rutherford House)

    2001 'Fundamentalism and the Christian Mission' in Partridge, Christopher (ed), *Fundamentalisms* (Carlisle: Paternoster Press), pp.263–78

Speer, Robert E. n.d. 'Foreign Missions or World-Wide Evangelism' in *The Fundamentals*, Volume XII (Chicago: Testimony Publishing)

Stephens, Prescot. 1998 *The Waldensian Story* (Lewes: The Book Guild)

Storrar, William Forbes. 1995 'Marrying Wisdom and Witness – A New Foundation for Practical Theology' in *But Where Shall Wisdom Be Found?* (Aberdeen: Aberdeen University Press), pp.72–80

Tagore, Rabindranath. 1986 [1912] *Gitanjali* (London: Macmillan)

Tawney, R. H. 1961 *The Acquisitive Society* (London: Collins/Fontana)

Taylor, William D. (ed). 2000 *Global Missiology for the 21st Century – The Iguassu Dialogue* (Grand Rapids: Baker Academic)

Turner, Victor. 1969 *The Ritual Process* (New York: Aldine De Gruyter)

Understanding Global Issues n.d. 'Superpower: American Military Dominance', No.100

van den Berg, J. 1956 *Constrained By Jesus' Love* (Kampen: J. V. Kok)

Verkuyl, J. 1978 *Contemporary Missiology: An Introduction* (Grand Rapids: Eerdmans)

Walls, Andrew. 1985 'Christian Expansion and the condition of Western Culture' in *Changing the World* (Bromley: MARC Europe)

    1995 'Christianity in the Non-Western World: A Study in the Serial Nature of Christian Expansion' in *Studies in World Christianity*, 1:1, pp.1–25

    1996 *The Missionary Movement in Christian History* (Edinburgh: T & T Clark)

    1999 'The mission of the Church today in the light of global history' in Martinson, Paul Varo (ed), pp.386–8

    2002 *The Cross-Cultural Process in Christian History* (Edinburgh/New York: T & T Clark/Orbis Books)

Ward, William. 1821 *Farewell Letters* (London [publisher unknown])

Warren, Max. 1951 *The Christian Mission* (London: SCM Press)

Wessels, Anton. 1994 *Europe: Was It Ever Really Christian?* (London: SCM Press)

White, John. 1993 *Money Isn't God – so why is the church worshipping it?* 2nd ed (Leicester: Inter Varsity Press)

Wilson, Derek. 1997 *Hans Holbein: Portrait of an Unknown Man* (London: Phoenix)

Wood, Michael. 2000 'Paths of Glory, Paths of Shame', *BBC History Magazine*, 1/7, November, pp.14–18

Yates, Timothy (ed). 2000 *Mission – An Invitation to God's Future* (Calver, Sheffield: Cliff College Publishing)

Index